On Bicycling:
An Introduction

On Bicycling:
An Introduction

An essay by Samuel Atticus Steffen

Serpent Club Press

ON BICYCLING: AN INTRODUCTION
Copyright © Serpent Club Press, 2014
All rights reserved

Serpent Club Press books may be purchased for educational, business, or sales promotional use. For more information please contact Serpent Club Press at theserpentclub@gmail.com

First Edition

Printed in the United States of America
Set in Williams Caslon
Designed by Emily Gasda
Edited by Kelly Swope

ISBN
9780990664314

LCCN
2014947744

A Word of Introduction to
"An Introduction"

In April of 2011 four young college graduates—Bill Cranshaw, Paul Cavanagh, Hannah Liddy, and Sam Steffen—set off from Irvine, California on their bicycles, heading East, with the intention of arriving at Ocracoke Island, off the coast of North Carolina, sometime in June of the same year. Their intention was to cross the United States on their bicycles. Their journey was cut tragically short, however, when one of the riders, Bill Cranshaw, was struck by a car and killed just outside of Searcy, Arkansas, forty-five days into their trip.

In addition to being riders, all four companions were also writers, and each kept a personal journal for the duration of their journey. The following is an essay that was written by one of the travelers upon returning from that trip. It was intended to serve as the prelude to his journal, to situate for the reader the context and mindset of the individuals involved in the journey, as well as to propose an argument advocating the bicycle as the best means of available travel. This will hopefully explain the title.

Because telling the story of the trip and explaining the motivations for going are each lengthy enterprises on their own, and because the tones of each have become so radically distinct as a consequence of the circumstances surrounding the adventure, the editors have decided to publish the following essay as a stand-alone work. The journal itself, which narratively outlines each day of the trip at some length, has not sought publication here. This will explain why the essay alludes several times to a forthcoming text which is not, herein, forthcoming.

On Bicycling:
An Introduction

When I wrote the following pages, or the bulk of them, rather, I lived on the open sea of the road in these United States of America. I had no vehicle for my transportation other than a bicycle which I had taken the trouble of learning how to disassemble and reconfigure, as par to the course of the haphazard nature of experience—and the will to travel, of that variety that is uniquely the cyclist's own. I lived not as a beggar, nor as a rambler, nor entirely as a tumbleweed—though for forty-five consecutive days I was made to contend with the grace, the compassion, and the irrefutable kindness of strangers. I was not adrift, as so many highway and cross-country travelers have made themselves out to be; neither was my purpose so clear and definite that I had my way all mapped out before me, and could count my experience, for how carefully I had imagined it, hardly worth the trouble of writing down. When I wrote them, it was in transit between the cities of Irvine, California and Ocracoke Island, North Carolina, along the Outer Banks, near Kitty Hawk, where the infamous Wright Brothers made their first historic flight. I wrote not because I knew very well what I should find out from my experience in traveling, but rather because I did not know at all. Before I had made my departure I was certain only of the fact that if I were to accomplish the goal of traveling such a distance with only my bicycle to carry me and only my strength to go on, I should certainly have liked to have had a way of telling someone about it, and fully, lest the adventure of the journey, which I could not anticipate before I had let myself go and have it, and which it has become my heavy task to narrate now, be lost to what should have been only the satisfaction of the achievement—that is, the sense of being finished with something, merely because I had returned.

To try to say now what my intention was in making such a trip by such a means—when I knew all along that more than half of my intention in going was to decide my reasons once I had taken some significant steps towards their completion— should seem unfaithful to an account that has tried to take its time to preserve ignorance where it was present, shame where it occurred, fear where it descended, and love where it endured. The foresight of hindsight always pretends to know too much; the hindsight of foresight is merely reluctant to relate the many secrets it contains. That being said—I do not believe I was entirely without my reasons.

For one—until I had made the trip, I was entirely ignorant of what certain parts of these United States even so much as looked like, in spite of having lived all my life in them, all the while calling them my home. I do not know if this circumstance will immediately strike my reader as absurdly as it eventually came to strike me, though I am quite sure I am not the only one among the citizenry here who suffers from this handicap in his experience. In fact, I will go ahead and presume that I am in the very large majority of the American population in this affliction. For our belonging to one of the most advanced industrial nations on the planet, and for having, by default, what is arguably one of the best, and most extensively well-connected systems of roadways in the world—I can hardly help saying that we Americans do remain a sadly undertravelled people on our home field. This is hardly anyone's fault; we might entirely blame the geography. I have heard of a certain South Pacific Island that is an entirely independent country and has for its area a comparatively manageable, and even meager eight and one-half square miles of land to accommodate its estimated 13,000 resident citizens. Imagine! With a geography like that I almost think it should be possible to make a walking tour of the entire country a part of one's daily exercise—and be done with the national circumnavigation before the midday meal. What an unfathomable enterprise for the American—who, I am convinced, at whatever age, could easily spend the rest of her days adventuring solely upon her native ground and, like the lightning bolt, never find that she had struck upon the same place twice.

But though we blame the massive and diversified geography of this country for the unreasonableness of that plan that should have us attempt to visit and acquaint ourselves with its entirety, we ought not to overlook the benefits of undertaking that project in small part, the part of which we may come to find, after all, contains something like a whole, if only in the trying. Before I went, I had never seen the Great Plains, nor felt the swelter of the deep south; I had never perceived in all their cloudless glory the stars over the Mojave desert, nor smelled the orange groves of southern California; I had not touched the Pacific Ocean (had never so much as seen it, save in pictures and in film), had never been to, and could not have fathomed any reason why I should ever find myself with a suitable occasion to visit Goffs, California; Tucumcari, New Mexico; Stinnett, Texas; or Hulbert, Oklahoma. Yet what occasion, afterwards, became more suitable than that I happened to be traveling upon a road that took me through them? And why did I find myself upon that road, but that I had decided it was the best way to get where I was going? And where was I going? And from whence was I going there? I tell you, there is nothing like a journey composed of two arbitrary, unknown ends, to give all the middle something like a purpose.

In fact, before I had set out on my adventure, I had never been further west in the country than Santa Fe. This will come as something of a surprise, I'm sure, to those of you who have spent the better part of your lives in Santa Fe, or within a stone's throw of it, or otherwise west of it, and have nourished such a strong admiration for that part of the United States that you have never felt any desire to travel east of the Sangre de Cristos. For myself, this limitation that had been placed upon my western reach was considerably owing to my circumstance, and had little to do with whether or not I should have liked to have visited the western part of the country before I did. I was born in Duluth, Minnesota—but this is irrelevant—and was shortly thereafter moved to the little town of Bethlehem—an old Moravian stompinggrounds in eastern Pennsylvania where I was entirely raised. Bethlehem had been rather well known as one of the centers of the American steel industry in the early 1900s, but by the late 1990s—right about the time I had come into some of my most formidable years—the industry, with the whole town around it, had fallen into practical bankruptcy and disrepair. It was not until several years after I had brought myself finally to quit Bethlehem, and to do it with a sense of committed permanence in the leave-takings, without knowing in the least what I should find ahead of me, and knowing only too well what I meant to leave behind—that I finally discovered I had not only reason, but maybe even *need* to do it. I do not know if any understanding of this necessity can be properly expressed, except in hindsight, by way of some very tedious description of all the people whom afterwards I met with, the places I saw and lived in, the experiences I had, and all the things that happened to me once the thing was done. I will spare the reader the extensive details of my biography, as the present narrative is concerned primarily with much more recent and particular events; however, let it be said that there is perhaps some analogy here to be drawn between what inarticulable reason I had for leaving my first home in the twilight of my adolescence, and that mysterious willingness I had for endeavoring upon such a trip as the one I have herein to speak of.

Before I went I had never spent the night in any National Park or stranger's home or Native American ceremonial hut, nor taken any serious notice of what a beautiful and geographically diverse place these huge and vastly independent-seeming but still-United States are—of what magnificent people there are to meet within it!—of what glorious assortment of birds and endless catalogue of flora and fauna! Indeed, I never was an American until I merely went to see, the first time, the country I have always called my own. And if there needs must be a reason for my going, let it be, quite simply, that by my twenty-second year, I had not done it yet.

The thought has since occurred to me that perhaps my initial ignorance of these so-called places was not entirely my fault: after all, I can hardly help it if I was born into a country so vast that it must span more than a fifth of the planet's twentyfour timezones. Tell me: what does any country need with more than a single timezone? I have heard a lot of palaver about the necessity of the timezones for the regulation of commercial transportation and industrial trade. But what, after all is so regular about it? Determined geographically, a single hour may spread itself— in America, anyway—anywhere between 700 and 1,500 miles, give or take a few. Regular?—That's 800 miles of geographical disparity! Regular!— Consider, my dear reader, how, on any given day you may travel south and west from the little town of Van Buren, at the Northern tip of Maine—the anthropomorphic eye and brow of the great weird animal of our country—to Evansville, Indiana— at the proverbial "foot" of that middle-American state—without ever losing the natural hour of the day in the transit. Observe: when it's seven o'clock in Van Buren, according to the National Clock of Washington D.C., then it's also bound to be seven o'clock in Evansville—and that pretty much holds for anywhere and everywhere in between. The geographical space between these two places makes for a ground distance of something like 1,180 miles, depending on your route. While this fact may not seem too remarkable of itself, yet, when compared with another traveler, who, let us say, for the sake of continuity, is also heading in a westward direction, from the town of Clovis, New Mexico to Bullhead City, Arizona, who is able to cover no more than 730 miles before he or she inevitably passes out of the timezone altogether—the disparity between a 1,180 mile-hour and a 730 mile-hour is bound to seem egregious. How to account for it? Is the sun so well-read of the Eastern States that it may skim them over in its daily read-through, a little bit faster than it may do with any of the Western ones? Is this why the sun seems to stand completely still for longer hours in the desert of the Mojave?—because the same amount of sunlight is devoted to the 730-mile southwestern-American hour as the 1,180-mile northeastern-American one? Of course not! The sun does not care what part of the world it sees: it shines with equal care upon them all. What irregularities exist—they must be, and are our own invention.

Yet it is difficult to conceptualize a mile-hour. Of course we are used to seeing miles given over a rate of time, as time passes. How fast we are going is usually (in America, anyway) expressed in miles-per-hour—at least it is in most of our automobiles. Conversely, it is rather difficult to consider time frozen, as it is bound to become when it is given a geographical dimension. But of course a mile-hour is not merely a unit of time, after all—nor is it merely a unit of distance. Say, rather, it is a unit of geographical distance, considered as having a temporal dimension.

Now, holding this in your mind, let it be said that by the time I had turned twenty-one years old, I had spent twenty-one years upon the North American continent having experienced only a very small portion of its geography. It had not occurred to me before this time that my entire life's experience might be cast in terms of a few crowded square miles, the none of which I had been allowed to take for myself as my own. There are times, reader, when, in some instance of a long reflection, an individual may look back on his or her life-to-date and be amazed that it has gone the way it has so far; when it may seem that everything that one has ever done with and within one's time has amounted to the consequences of his or her circumstance, and nothing else; when one realizes that one is really only here upon the world for a limited time, with a piece of life that one has hardly given much thought to trying to sculpt in any particular way, which has only come to look the way it has because of forces and agents beyond the individual's control that have acted upon their putty-object without any rhyme or reason, and have met with no resistance whatsoever in the process. So that those qualities of character and talent and interest and skill which one has developed in one's individuality begin to seem one's own merely by one's proximity to things—that is, merely by chance. And this chance, once recognized, begins to seem the true state, the terminus and origin of one's whole existence. For so too are there times when one knows all too well that one has not asked to be brought into this world, that nobody has asked for it; that nobody, being in it, may be exempt from death; that all human life stands as a kind of abandoned project which, having insufficient time to either solve or complete, must be simply passed on to posterity (through an act of love) in the hopes that what is issued may gain the experiences of their predecessors in one way or another, and learn to forgive them in the meanwhile work of living meaningfully themselves. But what a gamble it is! And how it may pain one to wonder of the extent to which one has ever really acted for oneself! The reflexive spasm to such a realizations as these, reader, of course, is to tighten one's grip upon whatever chains one feels, whatever reins one holds, to jerk them in any direction that one can, in order to know for certain the extent to which the vehicle upon which her life so far has ridden is the same one she has been driving all the while.

This was also part of why I went: I took up my bicycle for a long journey because I wished to claim something for myself, for the first time, to finally be somewhere for nor reason other than because I had put myself there, to move for no reason other than because I wished to. The fact remains that no human being, unless he or she is travelling at aggressively accelerated speeds from what is considered humanly possible, is really capable of experiencing first hand this discrepancy in geographical time I have been talking about. And I suppose, by this discrepancy, what I am really talking about is nothing other than what we who travel by airplane across multiple time-zones have become accustomed to referring to as jet-lag—i.e., the feeling that it is a certain time of day when it is actually another, owing to the sudden dislocation of one's person from one's normative geographical surroundings. There is a theory which holds that the greater distance traveled in a given amount of time, the greater the jet-lag will be. But is there not also a kind of jet-lag that may make one feel that he or she has been entirely dislocated from his or her age in history, from one's place in the world—a kind of jet-lag of the soul? I say that there is, and that this metaphysical disorder is what plagued me in the months preceding my trip. When I emerged from college, I was given by my circumstance to feel time geographically, and geography, temporally—insofar as either of these may be most easily felt by one who is either moving at ridiculous speeds across incredible distances, or has otherwise become entirely paralyzed by his or her constraints. Faced with a virtual infinity of options of where to go (anywhere) and what to try to do (anything), I became frozen with indecision. It seemed to me that to move without cause to Alaska (where I should have been acquainted with no one) should have been as reasonable as staying put right where I was. Of course it should have been my preference that nothing change at all, that I stay on for another year at my little college, and worry about what to do afterwards after another year of my life had been given to reading and discussing with like-minded individuals the art of writing. But to stay, when there was a grand, imposing feeling that one simply *ought* to be moving on—how could it be justified? It seemed that things were suddenly without their reasons, and whatever was to happen next, I must be the arbiter of my own destiny.

Now I have said that one of the primary reasons I had for wanting to make a trip of this kind was to see the country. This may satisfy my reader well enough. "But why a bicycle?" you will say. "Why not take a car? Surely you're not without access to some sort of automobile? Or a train? Better yet an airplane!—Why, you could see the whole country in a jiffy from an airplane window!" Yes—you are thinking. You understand the motivation, well enough—it's the means you can't quite figure. Perhaps it should be necessary, then, to mention here a word or two about the bicycle and what exactly is so befitting about this contraption to the wanderer who is in search of a journey. For it remains a personal conviction of mine that the bicycle is as much a means of transportation as it is a motivation to travel, all its own. And inseparable from one another upon this trip were the desires both to see the country, and to see it from "behind the handlebars," as it were.

Before proceeding, however, it behooves me here to amend a statement I made earlier concerning the undertravelled character of the average American citizen. This is only an accurate proscription provided the reader has the same understanding of the infinitive "to travel" that I have. The United States Travel Association (USTA)—which, I assure you, exists, and curiously enough defines itself in terms of its own corporate expansion as "the unique national organization that leverages the collective strength of those who benefit from travel to grow their business beyond what they can do individually"—has released several statistics in recent years that will refute our general American "undertravelledness" in one sense, and quite confirm it in another. For instance, that 42% of American adults traveled by air for leisure trips taken between August of 2008 and July of 2009 suggests that not only is almost half the nation's adult population getting around, but that it is getting around to destinations that are more than a skip away[1]. Paired with this, the fact that 76% of "leisure travelers" travelled by automobile "for leisure purposes" during the same time period, and that the airplane (which 42% of the American adult population utilized) was actually the secondary means of "travel" suggests that more people are getting around these days at some time in the year than remaining at home. Indeed, there is no one in America who is not in some sense a traveler anymore. In our twenty-first century American life, we are, all of us, becoming very well-travelled.

---

1 http://www.ustravel.org/news/press-kit/travel-facts-and-statistics.
  8 May 2012.

The common twenty-first century American utterance of the word "travel" bears connotations nowadays which bring foremost to mind the relaxing nap one may take between swims in transit from California to Hawaii aboard the Carnival cruise ship, the wide variety of cocktail- and soft-drinks from which one is asked to choose aboard the two hour coach flight from Nashville to Dallas, the infinite number of satellite radio stations from which to determine one's preference on the drive from New York City to Orlando in an air-conditioned cab—brings to mind, if anything, a sense of ease, of escape from "the everyday." Even if these are realities we cannot afford to enjoy ourselves, we are at least aware of the ideal possibilities of "leisure traveling". Granted, that this is how "traveling" rests upon our consciousness is probably as much the advertiser's fault as it is the consumer's. I would stress here in all of this (as the advertisers would probably, as well) the apparent "freedom of choice" one has in deciding upon the means of travel, which is, of course, a choice that will determine how comfortable one will be while traveling, and will depend, obviously, upon how much money one is willing or able to pay in order to "relax," to "be comfortable." Indeed, one is as free to spend one's money as one wishes in this country, just as one is free to make it however one can. But nowhere in the public sphere is the American income-gap more manifest than in the travel industry. A certain political correctness has descended upon us everywhere with regard to economic class, so that it is still considered impolite to ask even a very close friend: "So, how much money do you make a year?"—yet, first class passengers are still called to board first upon every airline in the nation, while the coach passengers are asked to please step aside, and be patient, as they gaze disgustedly or otherwise disinterestedly on.

Associations like the USTA, whose business (so far as I can tell) is to make traveling *look* comfortable, relaxing, much-needed, and in some cases even *virtuous,* have made it virtually impossible to consider traveling on any terms other than "business" or "leisure." There is no other kind of trip to make any more that is not for one's job or for one's relaxation therefrom. The notion of traveling which the industry has adopted implicates a meaning that is quite distinct from what it used to be. The word "travel" originally meant, and still means, "to make a journey." But it used to rhyme more easily with "travail," that is, "to toil, to labor, to suffer." In the fourteenth century, these two concepts were the same: all traveling was originally "travailing". There was nothing leisurely about it.

We might briefly exercise our imagination upon this notion of "travailing," insofar as it may help the reader understand the kind of traveling I am talking about when I say that we are undertravelled in America. I would emphasize here the immediate kind of suffering that is implied by the notion of travailing, as opposed to, say, the more permanent kind which involves acknowledging the very real pain of an unfathomable existence in whose trajectory is preserved the possibility of its having all been for nothing. The immediate suffering I speak of refers to the physical act of carrying all of one's necessaries upon one's immediate person or vehicle—i.e., to suffer, "to carry." This kind of suffering remains today an aspect of all traveling, but it is an aspect that the means of a comfortable transportation itself disposes of. We carry our belongings in suitcases only from the house to the vehicle, and from the vehicle to the station platform. When the train arrives we throw our luggage in an overhead compartment, or on a vacant passenger seat, and are allowed to forget about it for a while. The train does our travailing for us, while we are allowed to watch the countryside pass. But the mind reels to look at this too long. One sleeps, or grows bored, and reads the nearest magazine that can be got hold of. A traveler who does not carry her own luggage, who is not the primary means by which her necessaries are transported is in effect reduced to being nothing but a piece of luggage herself. Of course, as a paying passenger one is not required to pay attention to the traffic, or to the direction in which one is moving at a speed that is faster than any living creature can travel on its own—one need not feel guilty about this. This is part of the "comfort" promised by traveling by way of any public means anymore—that one's safety is entirely out of one's hands. If the train derails or the plane crashes, the passenger may be satisfied that at least it was not his or her fault. One either is or *must be* satisfied to know that someone else is paying attention to all of that. In effect, the passenger has paid his or her money so that he or she doesn't have to—so that he or she can *be passive.*

The problem I find in traveling this way consists partly in the lack of variation that should result from the actual experience of traveling as comfortably as possible. One's experience of the landscape from thirty-thousand feet and a thousand miles per hour is, I would argue, impossible to discern. To be glued to a window of a passing countryside is not unlike watching a television turned to the same channel. One really need not have left home at all to see it. The transparent separation of the traveler from the land over which she travels should only result in the eventual exhaustion of her interest in the scrolling panorama. When the body is at rest, the mind cannot but do its best to vary its thoughts a little. And when the body is at rest over a considerable interval, or better yet, when it has been persuaded that it has been made exceedingly comfortable for an inestimable duration—it will begin to suffer from a certain kind of discomfort that is caused by nothing else but the very things that were supposed to have made it comfortable. Even if one has, at the last moment, paid fifteen extra dollars to be afforded another foot of legroom for the duration of the flight (which it is actually possible to do now, on some airlines), the price shall not seem to have been worth it, after six hours of trying to sit still in a single place with a belt strapped about the waist. There is in human nature a tendency to change in spite of wanting to. Upon airplanes, there are those passengers who will get up to use the bathroom, merely to have an excuse to stretch their legs, even as there are those who, in spite of having full bladders, will keep their seats so as not to contribute to any sort of disruption in the pretended calm through which things seem to go. These kinds of discomfort which all passengers must endure who travel by plane, and train, and car, and bus may certainly be classified as a particular variety of suffering, but of a variety, I would say, that is more masochistic than not. The determination to travel by plane is admittedly not about trying to see all of what there is to see. With the ground so far below and the geography of the clouds to wonder on, what difference does it make whether one is situated beside the window or occupies an aisle seat? It's mainly about getting where one means to go as quickly as possible so that the time of travel can be reduced to a minimum, and the experience of one's destination maximized. Everyone is more or less agreed upon that. When such are the ideal circumstances, the best way to travel, admittedly, is unconsciously—absorbed either in a captivating distraction or else a long, deep, and dreamless sleep. And this, it seems to me is the main trouble: that, by and large, the best thing for the contemporary traveler of a thoroughly modern means is not to feel that he or she has had to move at all.

What is more, we seem to have a rather damaged confidence in our going for the going's sake— nowhere, anywhere, and everywhere—of making a very definite and specified departure, lacking any sort of definable reason for our journeying and feeling need of none. I cannot pretend to know what has been the cause of this. Perhaps part of the reason we are not better travelers in our own home country, is because we are not better tourists in it, either. Even for the increased exposure to my country which my experiences traveling undeniably yielded, I admit, I remain still vastly ignorant of its many greater parts. If anything, I am now only more aware of what a lot of roaming I have still to do before I have obtained even a very general understanding of what it should be possible to actually experience in this country, as an American—and that I have veritable miles to go before I have even a loose handle upon what fraction of the near-billion definitions we have in these United States for "home."

But this kind of consent which is involved in agreeing to be a passenger has always troubled me. I seldom fly, but I would have the reader know this about me: that I am incapable of climbing aboard an airplane anymore without having first talked myself into hysterics over the possibility of the plane's malfunctioning. I am never entirely certain that I will survive an airplane ride. Before take-off I cannot refrain from imagining the eight or so minutes that would elapse between a mid-air power failure and the collision with the ground in which I should have to reconcile myself to the irrefutable knowledge that *this is how I am going to die*. I am always disconcerted by the sight of fellow passengers who climb aboard and are immediately put to sleep by the near and heavy drone of a jet-engine. I must ask myself how anyone can sleep when I have just written several drafts of my last will and testament. Furthermore, I am bothered by the cool and easy manner in which the airplane safety is ever reviewed, with the false grinning of the flight-attendant manifest as he or she applies the oxygen mask and pulls the string in effortless demonstration of the task, as though it were a game of charades we were getting ready for, rather than, potentially, our collective demise. In a sense, this idea of the eight-minutes, in which one is suddenly made sharply aware that he or she has been imprisoned by the comfort of the fuselage, and has been somewhat deceived by the advertised safety of the airline, should seem infinitely worse than any amount of suffering that one might have endured out upon the landscape, beneath the weathers and at the mercy of one's own energies (by the way: I haven't any idea why I think it should take eight minutes. This number is one I have chosen at random, and is completely arbitrary. Perhaps it would be longer. Perhaps it would be much, much shorter). For myself, I think that should the situation ever arise in which I should find myself passively seated aboard a plane that is only moments away from crashing, my thoughts in that moment should be ones of pure outrage and protest—not only with the airline, that it has failed to make good on its promise of transporting me safely and comfortably to my destination, but with myself, too, that in spite of its always having been right there in front of me, every second of the day, I was never moved to take the possibility of my dying seriously enough to consider this supposedly comfortable means of transportation a dire threat to my existence—and potentially as the very means by which it should be brought to an end. But there is little use in speculating upon matters of these kinds. There is actually very little over which we, our captains or our conductors, have any sort of control—the future is certainly not one of them.

But the kind of travailing in which one suffers to remain still and passive—even unconscious!—in exchange for more miles per hour remains a perverse notion to me. Travelers ought to take more interest in their suffering: traveling ought not to be so concerned with arriving on schedule. Perhaps it even ought not to be so concerned with arriving at all. Of course some readers will say, "But when one has such numerous responsibilities, and work all the time, and only a few vacation days in the year, it is hard to find the time to travel any other way but as quickly as possible!" To such a reader, I would only venture to inquire as to whether—when one has admittedly but one single life upon the world to live, and an unpredictable amount of time in which to try to make the most of living it—whether it should not weigh more in the scales of our experience, the degree to which we desire to remain conscious of the ways we suffer in the ways we move. What concerned me in this adventure, as a travailer of these United States, was not merely suffering to carry all the perishable necessities that I could manage upon my physical person, but suffering also to keep hold of the imperishable ones that came to me as a result of trying. This is the main difference between that variety of traveling that is concerned primarily with destinations, and that less familiar act of travailing that is concerned with remaining conscious while engaged upon the journey itself—namely, that by the former we easily yield ourselves to a clean execution of the plans we authored, while by the latter, we are yielded to a story we must character ourselves.

Now let it be said that I am no masochist, that I would actively seek out a means of suffering deliberately in recompense for having lived what has so far been a comfortable life. There is little sense in deciding to suffer for suffering's sake merely because one has not yet had to. But part of what I intended to do in designing upon a trip of the kind I wished to take was to break forcibly upon my knee the bounds and referents of my awareness of the world, to leave with a conscious deliberation the safe sphere of school and home that I had only ever known and dwelled within, and to try my best to look at the world as if for the very first time, with my eyes wide open, with my senses sharpened, and with a certain susceptibility to all of what it should be possible to accomplish and fail at within this enormous world, of which life is admittedly only part, where there is no true monotony and no pristine repetition. It seemed there should be as much adventure as drudgery in such an undertaking, perhaps as much danger as amusement. The point was to go and see: I wished to sever myself, if only for a little while, from those bonds of obligation in which we who participate in the academic's and the tradesman's and careerist's life, become entrenched, to exercise my as-of-yet unpracticed freedom to roam deliberately, to sweat for my own gain, and, in the most original sense of the word, "to travel" this free land.

For my personal belongings I took only what I could suffer to carry, which amounted to the following items, in addition to my bicycle:

1 backpack, in which I kept:
- My journal
- A pack of pens (black ink)
- Several envelopes
- 1 book of US stamps
- Two books (William James' *The Varieties of Religious Experience,* Joshua Slocum's *Sailing Alone Around the World*)
- Several AAA maps (for the states of California, Nevada, Arizona, New Mexico, Utah, Texas, Kansas, Oklahoma, Mississippi, Arkansas,

Tennessee, Indiana, Ohio, North Carolina,
West Virginia, Maryland, Pennsylvania, and
New York)
- 1 toothbrush
- 1 tube of toothpaste
- 5 spare inner-tubes
- Several patch kits
- Tire-levers
- Allen wrenches
- 1 bottle of chain lube
- 1 spare handkerchief
- Zip ties
- A Leatherman pocketknife
- 1 bottle of sunscreen
- 1 roll of duct tape
- 1 lighter

1 front bag, in which I kept:
- 1 seashell from the beaches of California (which
  I intended to carry from the Pacific to the
  Atlantic and toss in)
- 1 small notebook (for taking notes)
- The directions for the day
- Several tools
- A spare chain
- silverware
- Sewing kit
- A bag of trailmix
- 1 water bottle

2 medium-sized rear Pannier bags, in which I kept:

- 2 pairs of socks (in addition to the ones I was wearing) which sometimes seconded as gloves in higher altitudes
- 1 pair of jeans
- 1 pair of running tights
- 1 spare t-shirt (in addition to the one I was wearing)
- 1 sweatshirt
- 1 rain poncho
- Spare spokes
- Extra 5-gallon ziplock bags, for storage
- A large quantity of food, the store of which was exhausted and refilled periodically
- 1 sleeping bag
- 1 sleeping mat
- Several bungee chords
- 2 gallon water jugs
- 2 spare water-bottles

Now: As there may be some readers among us to whom the very idea of bicycling—never mind what distance—should seem as foreign to their capacities as speaking the language of another country; who will regard the bicycle as a distasteful and outdated mechanism, and reject it with a considerable degree of fear and mistrust either because they cannot ride one and simply believe they do not wish to, or else have let their hearts harden against the activity by any number of arguments and first-hand experiences which they have so far met with in their travels—I can think of no better way to commence or to proceed with such an explanatory as we have here proposed, than to preserve the views and perspectives of those who may be sitting now in ready disagreement with us as the most-deserving of our attention. It is neither merely for politeness's sake that I say this—though I certainly intend no *dis*courtesy by it—nor entirely for fear that perhaps, in the course of denouncing another individual's opinions, I should, like so many politicians, come to find that my own beliefs had very little substance to themselves. Say, rather, it is because I like to think I am as ready to hear and entertain the arguments of others as I am to express my own—and that there is nothing that riding a bicycle may develop so well in one as the quality of a gregarious receptivity. That being said, let me see if I cannot "clear the air" a little around those innumerable misconceptions one is bound to have, who either does not currently own a bike or else does not immediately perceive its superiority to any and all other means of transportation.

Hence, at this time, I would invite any and all objections that have either historically arisen in this debate or that may now be invented by your best imagination against the enterprise of bicycling, to please come forward—that their existence might at least be acknowledged, before their legitimacy is set aside:

1. *Historically speaking, the need for the bicycle has become obsolete in our contemporary day and age of the car, train, jet-plane, and everything else we have to get around in.*

I have never met with anybody so utilitarian in mind-frame that he or she would actually suggest the preeminent obsolescence of the bicycle—but I am sure the argument has been made. Let me just say: Historically speaking, it actually makes very little sense to try situate the bicycle on a timeline of progressively-developed transportation. While it's certainly true that in its original conception (somewhere in the mid-to-late 1600s), the bicycle was intended to fulfill the role of a means of transportation that would be less costly, more efficient, and cleaner than anything else available at the time (which is to say, pretty much anything requiring the use of an animal)—the history of the development of the bicycle reveals that it never actually caught on in that way. Of course "intended" is not even the right word. Rather—let's say that the discovery of the bicycle was one of those providential accidents of the scientific method, wherein one hypothesis, being tried, and failing, necessarily led its would-be inventors on to rethink their methods considerably in developing another draft, and then another, and so on, interminably, until the result of error had yielded fruits it did not know it wanted. There is evidence that suggests that scientists and inventors were already looking into alternate energy sources with especial regard to the question of transportation as early as the seventeenth century. The barbarism of history which had kept the horses and mules of the Enlightenment in the bridle and the yoke was in dire need of some revision. One primitive solution to this "transportation problem" was the treadmill bus—a horseless carriage propelled by alternating foot-treadles, and steered by a driver. If you are not familiar with the treadmill bus, it is probably because it never quite caught on. History has clutched to the idea, though primarily in the blueprint. We may easily perceive that the conceptual difficulty in imagining such a vehicle is to be derived from the practical difficulty of operating it: in order for two men (they would have been men) to create enough propulsion to move the wagon, full up of people as it was intended to be, they would probably have both needed to be as strong as oxen, themselves, as prerequisite, and would probably have both been pooped in a quarter-mile. This answer could be no solution. It put a man in place of the animal—and the cart before him, too.

Then an eccentric German named Karl Von Drais came along in the early nineteenth century and invented a little thingumbob called a "draisine" which resembled pretty much what bikes are today, save that it lacked anything resembling crank, pedal, bottom bracket, chain, derailleur, cassette, brake, or shifter. It was essentially a sturdy wooden frame with two wooden, spoked wheels, a saddle, and a movable fork at the front, with handlebars for steering. To go, you merely pushed off the ground with your legs—and to stop you simply shoved your heels into the ground. It was also known as a velocipede. Its primary advantage was in traveling downhill. This did not catch on with everyone at first, either. The man who invented it rode it around like a curiosity and sold maybe one or two in his lifetime, at some exorbitant price. He supposedly made several cross-country trips with it in Europe, and could go something like 80 or 90 miles a day, which admittedly was better than anybody was doing who didn't have a horse to ride, or a carriage to ride in. But it needs saying that when this first pseudo-bicycle was invented, it was definitely *not* because it had improved upon the services of the horse-and-carriage that history decided to hold onto it. No—the reason history clung to the little contraption was primarily *because it was fun*—and even though time and innovation moved on, right past it, and the steam engine and the railroad were eventually built and installed everywhere, the bicycle did not fade, but only came more into its own. It's true it never had a place in the forward progress of industrial history. It is far more accurate to say that it cropped up in independence alongside of that progression. And there let it rest—for there is something really grand to me about the fact that the bicycle, historically speaking, was the product originally yielded in a process of looking for something better than what was available—and that it has become a sort of tool for engaging individuals in this same process today.

2. *Given the option between a car and a bike, I would take the car because it is much more "liberating" than a bicycle.*

More liberating than a bicycle?!—But I must take this commentary seriously, and do. Reader—are you at all aware that the bicycle was a great catalyst in the American sexual revolution? Indeed—for what could be more liberating than a machine that, at its earliest inception, allowed you to travel extremely great distances a) without risking the family carriage; b) without traveling accompanied by anybody; c) without wearing out your best shoes in the transit; d) without becoming completely exhausted; e) without paying for gas or feed or fuel; f) without emitting harmful toxins or, in the case of horses, a little thing I like to call 'poop-on-the-street'; g) without requiring permission to go; h) without having to tell anybody where you were going; i) without having to know yourself where you were going; j) without being dependent upon any person or animal other than yourself to get you there. In short, it empowered you in a way that just hadn't been possible before, and the main way it did that was by giving you a way to cover a lot of ground in a relatively short period of time, completely by way of your own energy. That meant, essentially, that you could get away from the people you wanted to be away from (ie—authority figures), and you could go and be with the people you wanted to be with (ie—friends, or, if the case so happened to be, lovers). The way sex fits into all of it is that now you and your significant other could get yourselves to a nice riverbank or patch of weeds or abandoned barn or what-have-you which was far enough away from your house and the house of your significant other where it wasn't likely either of you were going to be caught fooling around by one of your shotgun-toting fathers or switch-bearing mothers. And you could be alone for a while and watch the sunset and promise each other all sorts of wonderful and impossible things, and still be home in time for dinner. None of which had been possible before, when all you had was the school prom or the square dance at the church or the firehouse box social to keep you not only connected with your community, but under its constant surveillance, as well. Now you didn't even need your community. You could sort of come and go as you pleased. Or you could get a whole group of people together, and just go and start your own counter-culture.

The thing about it was though, the bicycle never really had its moment in the limelight before the automobile swooped in and sort of empowered us even more, and gave us not only a way to put a mile between ourselves and our authority figures in less than a minute but also a way to run them completely over, and outrun them, too—even beyond the sunset. (This is where we can lament rather than celebrate the fact that the bicycle never had a place on the timeline of linearly-progressive transportation, and never actually came to replace the cart-and-horse—whereas the car actually did). Here was a machine which you really didn't even need to know how to drive in order to be able to drive. Its empowering capacities were twentyfold that of the bicycle. A veritable upgrade. It was stronger, faster. It could carry several passengers. It could carry a lot of stuff, too. It had a radio in it. It had headlights so you could drive at night. You could bring food into it, and animals. You could pack up the whole family and go to the ocean for a long weekend. In many ways it was everything the early commercials said it was: a superior mode of transportation. Never mind that it was way more expensive than a bicycle, that within eighty years or so of its existence it had significantly diminished several of the planet's natural resources, that it contributed significantly to air-, noise-, water-, and light-pollution, a new sense of isolation and loneliness, as well as to a completely different kind of social disengagement than anybody had seen before or could have possibly anticipated: at least it could get you places faster, and with greater convenience. It made all kinds of new living situations possible. Now you could work in the city and raise your family in the suburbs. You could get a lot more done in a lot less time (so goes the argument). And as far as the sexual revolution was concerned—nevermind getting to the riverbank or the abandoned barn, like your parents had to do. All you had to do now was take the car a ways out of town and you could just do it in the backseat.

A good mobility has always been associated with empowerment in America. Capitalism's mass-production and advertising took hold of the automobile—in many ways—at the direct expense of the bicycle. Everybody got a car, and a garage to hang their bike in. And in America today, it's now the automobile that the bicycle has chiefly to compete with. The main point I'm trying to illustrate by all of this is that a reasonable mobility has always been a way for us to assert the freedom and the individuality we are always talking about in this country. The car and the bike both offer that—the car offers it, some say, to a more immediate and powerful degree, with a lot less physical energy required to cover a lot more distance in a lot less time. The bike offered it first, though—both historically, and today—to every kid who isn't old enough to drive, with a sweetheart, or a curious soul, or just a lot of energy to burn.

But let me just say: if you're really going to make the argument that a car is "more liberating" than a bicycle you have to be ready to account for how much money you're going to end up spending on purchasing the car in the first place, then on the gas it is going to require to keep it running, and the insurance you're going to be required to have in order to be able to drive it, as well as the innumerable repairs which you are going to need a considerable degree of specialized knowledge to be able to know how to 'fix' on your own, and which knowledge, if lacking, is also probably going to cost you. And you're probably going to want to have a good plan for how you are going to end up spending all the time you will no doubt "save" driving your car, rather than riding your bike, from point A to point B, which, I'm telling you, is still going to get spent, in the end, somehow—if not riding your bike, then waiting around to fill up your car at the gas station, or waiting around in a trafficjam, or waiting around to do something else, somewhere else. And you should probably also keep in mind that a good chunk of the money you're making at that job of yours is actually just going right back into the vehicle that gets you to and from work every day. And you'll have to be ready to account for all the moral responsibility you are going to have to carry with you for all the air and noise and light and water pollution you are going to be creating in driving that car of yours. And you are going to have to be ready to account for the way having a car gives you a whole lot of responsibility for not only getting yourself around, but maybe also for getting other people to and from where they want to go, too. Because all of those encumbrances are part of what you are getting in your "liberation" from the bicycle—which doesn't have any of them, and never will, because it can't.

3. *But you have to admit—bicycling really is much slower than driving a car.*

This one is true, I suppose, but only in a completely unqualified sense. It is also true the other way—driving an automobile really is much slower than bicycling: providing, of course, that the scenario is properly described. It could also be true that bicycling is much slower than walking, if the pedestrian knows a shortcut—through the woods, maybe—that the cyclist can do little about. It's also true—in this world of unqualified truths—that being much slower than a car really has no disadvantages whatsoever. But perhaps we are getting ahead of ourselves.

The problem, you see, with making statements like this, is that we don't really know what kinds of values might be lurking behind the vague and general and apparently-valueless observation about the automobile and the bicycle, and which is faster than which—because the values themselves, as well as the circumstantial variables that function as determinants for the truthfulness of the truth haven't been stated. Knowing only what we do, we might logically inference any of the following to be the intended meaning of the aforementioned observation (i.e.—that bicycling really is much slower than driving a car).

A. It is good and reasonable to travel by car whenever possible, because traveling by bicycle really is much slower than traveling by car.

B. It is good and reasonable to travel by bicycle whenever possible, because traveling by bicycle really is much slower than traveling by car.

C. Bicycling really is much slower than driving a car—when the two are racing, without regulations, a distance of 50 uphill miles.

D. Bicycling really is much slower than driving a car—when both drivers must individually transport two hundred pounds of oranges a distance of seventy city blocks.

E. Bicycling really is much slower than driving a car—when the bicycle has no wheels because they are in the car's backseat…etc.

My presumption is that, upon being asked *why* anyone should prefer driving an automobile to riding a bike, those individuals who will immediately defend themselves with the observation that a car is faster than a bicycle, or a bicycle much slower than a car—are aligning themselves with Formulation A of our aforementioned value-chart—and that the reason they agree with Formulation A, (it is decidedly good and reasonable to travel by car whenever possible) is not simply because the automobile will beat the cyclist nine times out of ten. It's because, more than beating the cyclist, the automobile beats every other means of transportation around it that can't fly. Of what any of us have available to us, it's not simply because the automobile is the *faster* of two available options that it gets picked so frequently. It's because it's *the fastest*. And the reason we want what's fastest has to do with another value that we hold pretty near and dear in this country: Time.

I am going to go ahead and presume that most Americans—like all forms of public transportation—operate on something like a time-schedule. Last I checked, a good majority of children, ages 5 to 18 are still going to something like school in this country—and most schools still have something like a beginning-time and a closing-time, at least five out of seven days in the week. And hopefully there's still something like a weekend to keep the schooldays separate from the non-schooldays. And I like to think that a majority of the population that isn't going to school (but maybe even including a portion of that population that is) is currently employed in some sort of work for which it is being given something it wants in return for its services or its time—money comes most immediately to mind, but I realize: there are other things than money for which some people work and live. Work, too, must have its opening- and closing-times, its starting- and stopping-times. So, too, must life: most of us probably know—though perhaps some of us don't, or would simply prefer it if we could forget it a while—that we are not long for this world, that we are all mortals here and someday shall die, and that our time here, however short or long it may prove to be, is a limited resource that may run out any time, really, we know not when. When contrasted with the moment of our dying, one's time, however long, even if it has amounted to a century, is bound to seem too brief—the swiftest and most fleeting thing of all. (Yet even if you had one moment more, would one moment be enough time to change your life? To say what needed saying? To do what should not have been left undone? I would ask the reader to think about this—as it is well worth thinking about.)

I must scrape here against the fact of human mortality only to point out that the desire for time, under certain conditions—such as those in which one is made to reflect seriously upon the inevitability of his or her own death—is insatiable. And it may take me a minute, but I am going to submit that this insatiable kind of time is the same kind of time that one gets—or means to get, and never actually does—when he or she says that he would much prefer to drive a car than a bicycle from point A to point B, reason being that the former will quite simply be "faster,"—because it will "save time."

Let's first of all be clear and say just what kind of time it is we're talking about here, because it seems to me there's an awful lot of room for confusion. I hope that part of what we're talking about is *time-of-travel*—that is, how long it actually takes us to get from point A to point B—and that the argument we're being asked to consider is the one that says it's best to take your car to get yourself between these places because taking your car is going to save you time. And by "save you time," I hope, even if we are not completely sure about the meaning of this phrase, and may understand it only insofar as it must bear some correlative to the practice of "saving money," that we are at least conscious of the fact that the kind of time we are "saving" by reducing our *time-of-travel* is definitely *not* being put away in a bank somewhere, to be used later, like maybe some of our money is, and that we definitely *won't* be able to just pull it out whenever we've run ourselves out beyond our means, and live off it as though it were a retirement fund. The time is always right now— and I hope we are at least aware when we talk about "saving time" that what we're actually doing is introducing a completely different kind of time into the equation, which, since it's already been said, we might as well continue to call by the name we have given it: *you-time.* Saving you time is actually saving *you-time.* And what is you-time, you are wondering?

You-time is pretty much whatever *you* want it to be. It's whatever you want to do with that fifteen or thirty-five or sixty-eight "extra" minutes you have "saved" by taking your car instead of your bike to work and to school and to the supermarket and to the Laundromat and back again. Which sounds pretty good, at first, I'll admit. With sixty-eight extra minutes added onto your day, what couldn't you do? You could learn to speak another language! Or finally learn to play the piano. You could spend more time with your family. There's any number of possibilities. The thing about *you-time* though is that it's actually pretty significantly constrained by all the other things you already have or want to do anyway. This is because our *time-of-travel* as an experience over which we *do,* it turns out, have some amount of control, never exists in itself, but is always inextricably tied to those experiences that come both immediately before and after it—namely, what we do at home, before leaving for school and work; what we do immediately upon arriving at school and work from home; what we do immediately before leaving for home again, from school and work; and what we do immediately upon arriving home again, after leaving school and work. In other words, the *time-of-travel* is bound to merge with other, let's call them "consequent" or "dependent" times—such as the time for sitting and making coffee, watching a bit of morning news, reading the paper, or chatting with the other people you may or may not live with. That's not to say that everything you have or want to do upon arriving home following a long day at work or school is going to be significantly determined by whether or not you have taken a car or a bike—there would be differences, I'm sure. If you had just spent an hour and a half biking fifteen hard miles you would maybe want to get a drink of water and take a shower in a way I'm sure you might not care to do if you had just made the same trip in a car. But what's significant about these little vestigial time-frames that stand out as the last things we do before we get behind the wheel, or the first things we do after we get out from behind it, is that they are the times during which we are most likely to actually experience—and I mean really experience, as a *feeling*—the time we have "saved" in opting to drive our car instead of ride our bike, if we are ever going to *feel* it at all. Because even though time is a universal notion—something we all use to give our lives structure and to coordinate ourselves with one another—*you-time* exists on a mostly subjective and primarily individual continuum. *You time* is all about *you*. And here it's important to acknowledge that the way time *feels* to each one of us is really very different from person to person, and that at different times, even if two or more individuals are a part of the same experience, they are very likely to be having very different experiences of the same experience, simultaneously.

I do not know if this requires an example—but one grows tired of speaking in general all the time. Just to give a better idea of what I'm talking about: We might consider the morning routine of a certain gendered individual who, in order to arrive at her place of work by eight o'clock—which she must do in order to meet the minimum requirement the management of the establishment has set upon her in employing her—has already determined, by some private and embarrassingly precise individual science, that she must arise every morning no later than five fifty-five A.M., sharp. This she does, let's say, quite simply because Said Individual, whom I hope we shall find not to be so very unlike ourselves, has certain things she likes to do in the morning, between the experiences of waking up and arriving somewhere "on-time," which habit and sheer personal preference have taught her she really ought to *try* to do. To account for the how and the why of each of them, individually, should require much more time than I am prepared to lend this hypothetical at present (for whether you will acknowledge it or not, I am also on something of a time schedule, even as I'm writing this—as I'm sure you are, as well, in reading it); hence, please let only a brief (though by no means a too-brief) catalogue, of said routine, of Said Individual, suffice. I've a hunch it will be a helpful tool in expressing this misconception about the bicycle and the automobile, when all's said and done.

Now, because Said Individual knows herself, and knows that she is very likely to hit the "snooze" of her alarm clock a few times before she actually musters enough wakefulness to sit up in bed, in order to be up by five fifty-five A.M., sharp, so that she can accomplish all of the things she is going to try to accomplish in the time she has before she must arrive at work at eight o'clock, she is going to set her alarm for five-thirty (we'll presume she has an alarm, and sleeps, at night, in a bed, under sheets). After sleeping through approximately five cycles of the mechanism—which goes off every five minutes after it is engaged—the first thing she tries to do at five fifty-five A.M. is go for a short run. Granted, what is a "short run" for her is bound to seem like a long run to us. To some of us, any running at all, first thing in the morning, before breakfast, and before the sun has risen, is bound to seem dangerous, insane, or merely excessive. But we are not here to judge or criticize. Our task is primarily to observe, for the present. So then—in order to accomplish this first task, this run, Said Individual first stands up out of bed, dresses somewhat quickly in the dark, (we'll assume her running-clothes have been laid out the night before, that she has running clothes) then is out the door (we'll assume there's a door). She does some preliminary stretching, of course, but this gets factored into the time she has reserved for the exercise. The route of the run Said Individual takes is itself a routine, of sorts.

She follows the same roads in the same way, every morning, passing all of the same places. Because she knows that there is something very uncertain about time and the way it is bound to *seem* to pass versus the way she knows it will actually transpire, the length of her run is determined not by time, but by a very objective distance. That is, she does not run for ten minutes and then turn around and come back whenever that ten minutes is up; rather, she tells herself she must run to a certain corner of a certain street that is always the same before turning around again and running back (and here we'll presume she lives in a place where there are streets and corners). This is not to say the time it takes her to accomplish the run is not itself a determining factor in this routine we are outlining: it is. The time it takes her to complete what is her "usual" run, in spite of the fact that its distance is always the same, always varies slightly. This she knows well enough. But she is not really so concerned with the time that she keeps a journal of it or anything like that. In fact, she doesn't even put on her watch before she leaves her house (let's assume she lives in a house and that she wears a wristwatch during the day, but that she takes it off to sleep)—because she doesn't really care what time it is, so long as she knows that she left pretty close to her usual time, and is feeling this morning pretty close to how she usually feels. And let's keep this notion in mind, that everything is well and good so long as things are going "as usual." Because in spite of the fact that the way one experiences time varies pretty significantly from person to person, and in spite of the fact that the "feeling" of time itself remains, from a purely external viewpoint, an entirely imaginary feeling—the extent to which one is able to actually feel or experience "saved" time, is always in relation to a world of pure potential, to a world whose entire future is assured because it contains the vital aspect of repeatability.

It is dark outside, and there is very little traffic. She is not a marathon runner, nor is she a professional athlete. The only reason she runs, she sometimes explains to people who ask her, is that it makes her feel good. Actually, what she really says— this Said Individual—is: "It gets me going. There's really nothing else that does." And this is really quite a humorous thing to hear, reader, because even as Said Individual says this about running—that it's the only thing that gets her going—she has also been known to issue the same phrase in reference to a good cup of strong black coffee, which she also makes in this routine of hers—but not yet. We're not quite there.

So she is definitely aware that the time it takes her to accomplish this run is bound to depend upon several things—upon things she has already done, so far, with her day, and what she has still to do. The run, she has already decided, cannot be too long because she has to get back and do several more things before she must arrive at work at eight o'clock sharp. But on the average, we'll say, she is usually back in her room again, panting and sweating, at right around six-thirty, A.M. Upon arriving back in her room, she begins to undress, still in the dark. Immediately after she is undressed, she takes a shower. Because I am a gentleman I would not presume to tell you what sort of ablutions Said Individual performs in this part of her routine—suffice it to say the water may be heard from the opposite side of the bathroom door, to run for approximately ten minutes, and she is finished with her shower by six forty A.M. This, of course, presuming she has returned from her run just when we say she has. Some mornings, I am sure, she is bound to return a little later than six thirty A.M, and that will push this shower back a little further, as well, maybe even as late as six fifty. Other mornings, perhaps, she finishes earlier. And here it may be a good idea to mention that even though the sequence of events which compose an individual's routine, taken altogether, may be said to possess that prized quality of repeatability, the way repeatability actually functions in a routine has much less to do with the mechanism of the clock and how proximate any particular activity's starting- and stopping-time stands in relation to the minute of the hour, and far more to do with the syntax of the actions themselves—that is, the way the actions stand in line in relation to one another. All of this is just to say that Said Individual really doesn't need to be checking the time to see to what extent she is on- or off-schedule. She possesses a sense of that— and it is her ability to sense the extent to which she is right on schedule that is going to determine how she feels when she deviates.

Now she will probably dry off in some way, and then dress herself (and it is here, let me remind you, that she puts on her watch, among other things). We will await her, patiently, in the kitchen (assuming, of course, that she has a kitchen to call her own).

She arrives looking very wakeful and feeling very good, for the run has improved her circulation and given her some considerable energy with which to greet and seize the day. This is all very well and good. All is very much as it should be— "as usual." In a short time she must be at work, but right now, arriving in the kitchen with the sun just peeking over the horizon, there is time to spare and spend however she wants. Her hair is still wet, but not dripping. It appears to have been brushed, but evidently not blown-dry or subjected to any electrical appliance of any sort. She wears no cosmetic of any kind, though a vague scent is emitted from her sudden presence in the room, of some sort of tropical fruit, which is no doubt the result of her preferred variety of shampoo, or soap, which we may presume she uses.

Now she makes breakfast, which, for Said Individual, always consists of a cup of black coffee, a cup's-worth of hot oatmeal with granola and honey added, and a grapefruit. Some mornings she is forced to eat other things (assuming she has other things), or else to do without one or more of the elements that should provide her ideal breakfast with some reality in the world. But when she has all the makings for it, and enough time to prepare and consume it, this is what she likes to prepare, as habit and practice have shown that this will be enough to get her through to lunchtime (which is at 11:45, where she works, let's say). For the coffee and the oatmeal both, she fills a saucepan halfway with water (she owns a saucepan) and lights the stove (it's an old gas stove, about which she is a little paranoid—to which, occasionally, maybe two or three times a month, she will get up in the night, after she has tucked herself into bed, and stumble to in the dark, to visit, just to see whether the pilot lights, burning somewhere beneath the four darkened stovetop ranges, may be seen faintly still to glow) and sets the one upon the other and waits for the water to cross the boiling point. Has she ever once timed how long it takes for her water to boil? No. Not once. But she has often used the time it takes her water to boil to determine her next several actions. Once the water is on, she grinds a handful of coffee-beans in an electric grinder (a gift from her father, whom she thinks of, always, precisely here, at this moment in her day, if otherwise at no other) and pours the grinds into a French press (which she acquired some time ago, let's say, at a yardsale). She gets down a bowl and gets out her oats and pours a cup or so of them into the bowl; she carves her grapefruit into two perfect halves (for she does it every morning, and has almost perfected it by now). These she sets upon a plate and sprinkles with brown sugar, which she has taken down from a nearby cabinet (there are cabinets). By now the water is ready, and she pours half of it over the grounds in the press-glass, and lets them rise and steam and steep, then pours a fraction of that amount of the remaining just-boiled water over her dry oats, until they rise in a similar fashion. She adds granola to the oatmeal, and whatever frozen fruits she has stored away in her freezer (this morning it is blueberries). Then she stirs the steeping coffee with a knife (why it is a knife, we cannot know— but it is a knife, today, as always), and after waiting a little insignificant interval, plunges it. Following this she pours herself a mugful, slips her steaming bowl of oatmeal onto the plate with the grapefruit halves (it is a fairly sized plate), takes out a spoon from the drawer (there is a drawer, containing silverware), then moves with plate of grape-fruit and oatmeal in one hand, coffee and spoon in the other, to her kitchen table (there's a table) where she sets everything down. On her table already (for she has done this before, remember, and there is already sense of things being ready again for them to happen the way they usually do) is a novel of some kind, which is her "breakfast" novel. For the benefit of our example we need not peer too closely over her shoulder to see the title or the author, so as not to offend or excite anyone's individual tastes or sensibilities. It is only important that we mention it is a novel. It is not a newspaper or a television set or an electronic device. It is an old fashioned, well-loved paperback book of the sort you might still find in a bookstore somewhere. It is not always the same book, granted, the one she reads in the morning, for Said Individual also belongs to time, and cannot escape it, even being merely an example, and she always reads books from beginning to end, over time, in the intervals she designates of her own volition for the activity of reading. She is always able to remember well enough, when she sits down here at her kitchen table, just where she was in the story, so that she can keep reading, picking up more or less right where she left off. Over time, even though she has less than an hour for reading and must also try to eat her breakfast in this time, too, she consumes whole books this way. There are other novels spread throughout the house—one in the bathroom (there's a bathroom), one on her bedside table (of which there is also one), and several others filling a rickety old bookshelf she has in her living room. One gets the idea that she is not the sort of reader who likes to carry all her books around with her, but that she never likes to be without at least one. One gets the idea from observing her that she is able to read several books simultaneously this way without feeling too overwhelmed, merely by placing these books strategically throughout her house, and that she has placed these books where she has placed them so that she may make "better use" of her time. And by this strange phrase, we can only mean that now, whereas before she had only some physical indulgence to take care of, more out of necessity, perhaps, than anything else, in eating her breakfast in the kitchen, or using the toilet or brushing her teeth in the bathroom, or lying in bed in her bedroom—now she has also something to engage her intellectually while she performs these other physically or hygienically-oriented activities.

And it is truly remarkable how many books she has actually successfully read this way! She has claimed, the friends of Said Individual have said, to have read all of *Don Quixote* over a period of something like two years, solely in the two separate two-and-a-half minute increments of her daily routine that were originally reserved for brushing her teeth. It came to be that the time she must spend on the one actually began to determine the time she wished to spend on the other, so that eventually she had to limit herself to reading only two full pages of text before the spit-and-rinse, sometimes allowing a little more, and sometimes a little less, depending on the length of a particular sentence. Her dentist has told her upon several occasions that she has perfect teeth. But how little her dentist knows about it! She is an avid reader, though, to be sure, this Said Individual. For however long it takes her to finish her breakfast, she spends the remainder of her time at the kitchen table, reading, until it is time to go to work.

And here at last we have come to it—does she ride her bike or take a car? We must decide which of these she has, and what are the benefits to either, and what are the particulars of her circumstance (as everybody's will be different, no doubt—but what all morning routines have in common is precisely their individual nature). For starters—as I hope to explain something about it in a minute—let's just that she commutes by bicycle. And let's also say that she lives far enough from her place of work that it makes for a less-than-short ride on a bike—i.e. that it is far enough away so that taking a car would, in fact, be "faster." Let's say she lives seven full city miles from her place of work, and that provided that she has no mechanical difficulties in transit, that she takes the route with the least amount of hills, and that the traffic is "moving" more or less, let's say that it takes her twenty-five minutes, on the average, to get to work, bicycling.

Now, since this is the case, Said Individual makes a point of trying her best to be out the door by seven-thirty A.M. sharp. This is to allow herself a small five-minute window within which she may arrive at her place of employment, having taken maybe a little longer than usual to make the trip, without being late. So, she reserves a small portion of her time for the getting-together all the things she may want to take with her, and putting on all the extra clothes that may be required for a transit of this sort. But this only takes about a minute.

And this basically exhausts us of our cycle of what we are calling Said Individual's morning routine. To recapitulate, the syntax presents itself thus: 1) Awake, 2) Run, 3) Shower, 4) Breakfast, 5) Read, and 6) Go to work.

Drawing from the aforementioned routine, let's say that one morning Said Individual awakes at her usual time, and carries out her usual routine to completion, all the way to the part where it is time for her to go to work. Let's say she is sitting at her kitchen table, reading, and has just arrived at the end of a chapter and is thinking to herself, "Well, this seems about as good a place to stop as any. I must be going now."

But today there is something different. Today she has full and unbridled access to a car. Perhaps Said Individual has owned a car all along, and has made it a very deliberate choice of hers only to bike to work, no matter what—unless there is some emergency. Or, say again, perhaps it was recently given to her as a surprise. Or perhaps it is not actually hers, and she has only been charged with keeping track of it for a while as a favor for a friend. Then again, perhaps not. Perhaps, in addition to all of these, there remains another set of circumstances that may explain how Said Individual has come into the possession of a vehicle all of a sudden, at this point in the narrative— if there are not in fact twenty-thousand. As unlikely as any imaginary explanation will sound, based upon what habitual practices we have thus far observed to be characteristic of Said Individual—still, in a world where almost nothing is impossible, we cannot very well deny any of them their circumstantial plausibility.

And let's also admit the possibility, while we are at it, that this morning Said Individual may be feeling a little more tired than usual; that her knees may hurt today; that she might have been up later than usual last-night and may not be feeling quite as energized as she is wont to feel around this hour; that her book, rather than bringing her to a very good stopping place, has actually just started to get really good, so good in fact that she has begun reading it out loud to herself and has maybe even begun to cry. In short, let's say there are a whole host of reasons that may justify her in wanting to take a car this morning. And because we have allowed that this is certainly plausible, however unlikely, let's just say she does.

Because Said Individual knows that her twenty-five minute commute by bicycle will be shaved down to about thirteen minutes in her car (depending, of course, upon how many traffic-lights she makes, whether there is construction upon any of the roads, her route of travel, etc.), the possibility exists here for our protagonist to actually experience, upon this threshold of a decision, the *feeling* of saved time. And at first, what a great feeling it is! Though little other than a privileged glimpse at strangeness—a kind of first kiss, almost—saved time allows a flurry of possibilities to rain in jubilant precipitation upon its beholder. "What couldn't I do with all this extra time?" inquires Said Individual to herself. "I could enjoy a whole other cup of coffee! I could finish this book!" As though she had tricked herself in order to gain a sense of surprise in addition to what little relief she could afford from the constant fluttering anxiety which persistently wishes to know to what degree it is on- or off-schedule, the saved time, it seems, is able to be enjoyed only to the extent that it permits one to act deliberately out-of-step with the established routine, whose every action, known by now only too well, has created a little path through life whereon what has been deliberately diminished is the possibility of variation. Saved time is variation; it is time that has not yet been designated, that nevertheless exists in such close proximity to time which *has* been designated, one does not have suffer guilt or anxiety over whether or not one has 'given up' the routine, which is not surrendered. In one's experience of saved time, the world of the possible follows in the world of the actual as closely as an afternoon shadow. Every action performed in saved time is performed in direct contrast to those actions and experiences of another possible world, a possible world whose possibility is so possible in fact that it can actually be known, even while it is not being experienced— known not as a dissonance—a thing with which the present moment has created a rupture—but as a harmony. Saved time is new time, time over which one possess the freedom to spend oneself without having to suffer the penalty of debt. The extra twelve minutes comes to Said Individual here as a free gift, for which she does not have to thank anyone, with which she may do almost anything.

If this example is not doing it for you, we might imagine this *feeling* of time I am trying to describe here to be next of kin to that which we have also experienced on such familiar occasions as the snow day, the meeting cancellation, and the misread work schedule—instances for which the subjective account of your immediate future, part of which you were planning on sacrificing anyway, in accordance with what civic duties you may owe to your environment as a citizen, a student, an employee, or what-have-you, has been changed rather abruptly, and unexpectedly, with no real negative consequence. You are simply given the day off, for whatever reason, and are told that business as usual shall resume tomorrow. This is not exactly time "saved," but it's time you've more or less "earned" without doing anything extra, and you can enjoy it as much or as little as you want to. Because to your mind it was always somebody else's time— and now (finally, for the first time, or once more) it's yours.

But what does Said Individual do? How does she spend this "saved time" of hers? Let us observe:

She turns the page, and goes on reading.

And here we must admit what a frightening thing is the possibility of variation, and, in the process, I hope, reveal what is the dangerous misconception underlying this mentality that would have us always choose the car over the bicycle as a means of transportation for the reason that a car is the "faster" of the two. This misconception is rooted in the idea that one is actually capable of saving the time, to spend later, which is actually being spent on the continuation of the present moment. Consider: If you have a routine for which you are able to factor in the time of transit upon a bicycle, you really don't need it to be faster. The line of reasoning that would have us believe that a car must be taken because a car is fastest removes any sense of enjoyment from the act of driving. Taken from this perspective, the automobile is purely a means of transportation whose only good is in its ability to get you where you are going. People suffer who drive cars—that is a fact. Look at them sometime. If you are a driver yourself, only consider how miserable you are, how frustrated, how unaware, and how angry! You hate having to park, having to buy gas. When you are pulled over by a police officer, it is never your fault. Nothing about it seems just. But nothing brings out the worst in us quite like driving does. In a world where it has becomes so unfeasible to consider the slower of two things the best possible option, to choose that means, in spite of its being slower, is to acknowledge that there may be more to traveling than merely getting where you are going.

So far we have spoken about "saved time" as something which is done deliberately out of step with a very set-in-mind notion of the routine. Now imagine for a moment the consequences of being dragged out of step with one's routine, by forces of accident or circumstance or emergency, and what a severe disruption this is likely to cause to one's sense of peace. Imagine, for instance, a morning for which Said Individual, upon silencing her alarm clock several times consecutively, accidently, in her semi-conscious fog, shuts it off entirely and rolls over for another five minutes of sleep, only to discover, some several hours later, that she has slept through an entire cycle of her routine and will maybe even be late for work! What a panic this should cause! In a violent rush seem to pass before her eyes the things she should have done this morning, but did not do! The world of the possible (where things are known for certain) unravels before her and sets her current body reeling. The sunlight softly pouring through her window in absolute silence strikes her far more offensively than the dire blaring of a fog-horn in her ear. The newness and unfamiliarity of it throws her into convulsions of panic and outrage. What swearing! What annoyance! In a haste she pulls on her dress clothes and leaves her house that instant, forgetting exercise, ablution, breakfast, calm and all. Her entire day she is out-of-step, and all day spends herself merely waiting for tomorrow.

It strikes me that several things about the circumstances of Said Individual and this experience of her "saved time" we have already described must be taken seriously, in light of its pseudo-fictional basis of her experience as an illustrative example— the first of which is the fact that even though we have elaborated several possible reasons, without settling upon any, that might explain the means by which Said Individual has come to be in possession of a car, disregarding any of the aforementioned generalities, the instantaneousness by which this option became available to her—"out of the blue," as it were—is the essential thing in the way of providing her access to the feeling of saved time. And this instantaneousness of availability yields itself immediately to another consideration, one that is perhaps still more crucial—namely, that this feeling of having "saved time" is one which can only exist occasionally, from time to time, as the exception to the rule. What has saved you time today will save you nothing tomorrow. To do it again should be at the expense of the comparison with the established routine, by which the feeling of saved time is the emergent result, and without which it were merely alteration of the routine. Which is to say: were Said Individual to adopt the automobile as her primary means of transportation so that she could save time with it, it would eventually cease to provide her with the feeling that she has saved herself any time at all.

In the case of the automobile v. the bicycle, then—let's be clear—the only way you're going to be able to actually experience the time you've "saved" in taking your car is if, in making the transit, you're able to hold on to the experience which you didn't have—that is, of riding your bike. You see, because this concept of saving "time" only has value when it's been located on a spectrum of comparative experience. And I know it's going to sound crazy to say this, but I'm going to say it anyway: the only way you are ever really going to be able to *feel* that you have saved any time at all in taking your car instead of your bike—the only way you are really ever going to be able to *enjoy* your extra sixty-eight minutes, or however long the discrepancy actually turns out to be, that has been your *reward* for driving, is if you have already been, or currently are, a bicyclist. Because it's only the bicyclist—who, presumably, has already carved out of his or her day enough *time-of-travel* necessary for bicycling so that the bicycling won't significantly interfere with anything else he or she may have going on—who is going to be able to feel any difference in arriving home sixty-eight minutes earlier than usual, in a car. Precisely because what is new and strange and different is always felt in contrast with some concept we like to hold onto of what is considered "usual." Perhaps the worst irony of this whole argumentative scenario is that it's hardly said-bicyclist who is going to see the point in changing over to taking a car, when he or she has probably already taken several deliberate steps to making it possible to ride to work/school as an option.

4. *Bicycling is an expensive hobby.*

Alright. Since the question of expenses has here been raised in reference to the "hobby" of bicycling, it behooves me to explore this perspective a little before attempting its dismissal—for it shall be of service to no one to try reasoning one side of an argument without first trying to understand, to the fullest extent possible, that of the other.

Once more, let us consider in what ways the above statement is defensibly true. It seems there is a certain culture which has sprung up around the notion of cycling as "a hobby," and it is true, no matter what tax-bracket you consider yourself a part of, this hobby can become very expensive. There are bicycles out there that will not sell for less than $12,000—easy. But then there are cars out there that go for multi-millions of dollars, and are never driven, and just sit around in warehouses collecting value and prestige in discretion among so much dust. I am just going to go ahead and say that what is traditionally most valuable tends currently to be least practically usable. I prefer a well-used thing to a well-preserved one; a free item to a cheap one; and would rather see a well-loved object remain in loving hands than sold into strange unkempt ones. By now every kind of trinket and doodad has been invented or re-invented to make cycling that much more of a consumer's commodity. If you are green to the culture of cycling, and your foremost inclination is to go to your local cycling store to equip yourself for every possible comfort and likelihood that you should potentially confront out there on the road, there is a very good chance that you will be not a little surprised and immediately overwhelmed by the amount of merchandise a bicycling-shop may be found to contain in excess to the bicycles themselves and their necessary disassembled parts. By now there are a variety of cycling socks and cycling shoes to choose from, cycling leggings and cycling tights, cycling shorts and cycling underarmor, cycling arm warmers, cycling gloves, cycling sunglasses, cycling jerseys and cycling hats, cycling kerchiefs and cycling lotions (for every kind of chafing), cycling foods and cycling water-bottles, cycling ointments and cycling oils, cycling locks and cycling tools, cycling powders and cycling magazines, cycling stickers and tapes, medicines, trainers, trailers, bags, heart-rate readers and monitors, speedometers, Global Positioning Systems, lights, battery chargers, etc. The list goes on. All of this is bound to seem confounding to the individual who is the least certain of what is actually necessary for the mere act of riding a bike anywhere. Confronted by such a lot of gear, one is bound to feel right off the bat a little too poor to invest very much in the activity at all. But let us dispel this notion once and for all.

I would like it to be kept in mind that what we are about in all of this hemming and hawing is not to argue the bicycle as the cheapest means of transportation, or the fastest, but to demonstrate its comparable optimality over all other forms of transportation in terms of its costs and benefits to the traveler, in order to reveal the suitability of the bicycle to that individual who, with the barest notions of a journey having grown up before him or her, has only yet to decide upon the means. Even the act of walking has its obvious advantages over that of bicycling—as does the car, the train, the jet engine, and the ocean steamer. In a certain sense, walking is the most natural of all animal activities.

Observe the newborn colt, lately born out of its mother's womb: what is the first thing it does upon touching the earth but stand right up, on its wobbly untried legs, and walk? Even humans are not so quick to get the hang of it. It is a significant feature of this development that the skill of walking in humans is acquired long before the faculty of speech is developed. I do not pretend to be a psychologist, but it is very probable that a strong correlation of a psychological order may be found to exist between learning how to walk and discovering one's capacities for speech. In most of us, the one is practically the prerequisite for the other. We do not get our words in this world until we have our legs in it. What is more, a very marginal discrepancy exists between walking and wandering, the latter of which is just walking without a destination. What is all of life, but one long walk from the cradle to the grave? Walking makes the best use of the imagination; it invites distraction. Walking is that experience that best acquaints an individual with his or her surroundings. It is the noblest form of human movement, that through which one's uprightness and mobility is most fundamentally manifest. I would argue that the best thoughts that have ever been thought have been thought on walks: It has been suggested that Kant first articulated to himself the categorical imperative while on a walk through his hometown of Königsberg, from which he never strayed more than ten walking- miles in the entirety of his life. We may infer from the book of Acts that St. Paul's conversion occurred upon a *walk* to Damascus. Thomas Jefferson, rationalist that he was, considered walking to be "the best possible exercise." Among the items contained in the Smithsonian National Museum of American History is Benjamin Franklin's walking stick, which was as component to his identity as a diplomat as to his bearing as a pedestrian...

But I need not continue with this line of argument here; the reader may imagine for him or herself the thousand other examples that may and *do* exist to support the claim that the least pedestrian individuals in the history of the planet have been its pedestrians. The bicycle, on the other hand, in existing as an object that has always been completely separate from the human individual, and was not even privileged with discovery until the late 1600s, has not enjoyed the infinitely long history that walking has, as a basic human exercise. And unfortunately it now belongs to a mass market where the activity of bicycling is easily associated with a thousand extraneous pieces of merchandise, the most of which, quite apart from enhancing the fun or the excitement of bicycling as an activity, only serve to make it a more technically complicated endeavor for beginners. But let me be clear: the excitement that is derived from the simple act of bicycling and the excitement that is derived from purchasing bicycle merchandise are identical emotional consequences of two very distinct hobbies. Granted, most bicycle-gear junkies probably enjoy riding their bicycles as much as people who don't know the first thing about how a bicycle even works; the only difference is that this former type of person probably enjoys talking at great lengths about his or her bike even while he or she is riding it. This overwhelming interest in the machinations of bicycling need not serve as prerequisite for enjoyment of the activity. The pleasure that may be derived from just-plain-bicycling does not consist in the bicycle as an end in itself, but primarily in the bicycle as a means of getting around. It feels good to ride a bike— to be outdoors, to move, to gasp, to feel the wind in your hair, and to see the world as it is, without being confined bodily to the cramped cockpit of an automobile, forced to sit in passengeresque stillness while the world moves around you, subjected to the noisy revving of your own engine and the smell of your own exhaust. Yes, there are so many things to buy for a bicycle that should you find yourself endeavoring to purchase all of them, you will also find yourself in the poorhouse—and soon. But let me say this, to those of you who would steer clear from the bicycle for fear of its expenses: the only piece of equipment you need to be able to ride your bike is your bike—trinkets and doo-dads be damned! In addition to this, just as a safety measure, I would also recommend a helmet, no matter whether the law says you must wear one or not. Reflectors or a light would also probably not hurt any, as they may make you more visible to pedestrians, vehicles, and other cyclists who may or may not be out there on the road with you; and you may want to carry a patch kit, in the event that you are beset with a flat tire, and maybe a portable air-pump, as well. These things, though they do cost money, are not expensive when contrasted with the time, personal energy, natural resources, and money that you will end up spending on your car. If my word upon this does not persuade you, let me provide you with another example, to illustrate my point more precisely.

Considering the essentialist's economics of the issue—for I would consider myself an essentialist, in bicycling and in other of my fascinations, as well—say that you are currently a pedestrian, without any ulterior means of transportation. You have a little bit of money and are debating whether to buy a car or a bike. Last I checked (at the *Wawa* gas station on the corner of Shoenersville Rd. and Eighth Ave in Bethlehem, PA, December 21, 2011, 11:08 PM) the price of regular, unleaded gas was $3.28 per gallon. This means little to an individual who is currently dispossessed of a gas-powered vehicle. But say you buy the car. And say you are not very wealthy (as I am not very wealthy—in many ways, I suppose, but least of all in an economic sensibility). By what stroke of good fortune you have found a used vehicle for $2,000, which you have bought with virtually all of your savings. The reasoning here being that having a car will enable you to get around town more easily, and will allow you to work two, if not three jobs, which will help you make more money, faster, so that you will not always have to be among that class of people that is considered, if only hypothetically speaking, "not very wealthy". Say the car is in pretty good condition. It has 50,000 miles on it, and gets nearly 30 miles to the gallon. You have not been swindled in your purchase.

Okay. Now let's say that everything has started out quite according to plan. You bought the car and you got your three jobs and you're working a total of 45 hours a week. Say you make $11.50 an hour at a place where you have 20 hours, $10.00 an hour at another place where you have 15 hours, and $9.75 an hour at job number three, where you work a maximum of 10 hours a week. This works out to an income yield of roughly $477.50 per week, before taxes. After taxes, just for convenience sake, let's say you're making around $450 per week, which translates to a little more than $1800 a month and roughly $23,000 a year, when you factor in sick days, holidays, and whatever else.

Now: your standard monthly expense are $500 for rent—utilities included—and, on the average, about $250 for food. That leaves about $1050 dollars for spending and saving. But now that you own a car—we have to be realistic—a good chunk of that money is going to go into your car. But how much? Let's just see: to get between your house and all of these jobs, as well as whatever extraneous errands you're trying to run between the grocery store and the Laundromat—let's just say you're traveling an average of 30 miles a day. With the car you own, that's a little more than a gallon of gas, $3.28 you're spending every day. That might not seem like a lot, especially because you're not buying it every day. Probably you're going to buy several gallons when you're at the pump and not worry about it for a while—at least until the fuel gage is crossing over into EMPTY. But over time this really adds up. In a week you spend roughly $22.96 just so you can get to work. That's roughly $99.49 a month, and roughly $1,193.92 a year. That reduces your monthly spending and saving money from $1050 to about $950.

But let's not forget how the price of gas is bound to fluctuate, and how, now that you've gone ahead and bought yourself a car, to see the price of gasoline go up a little bit is definitely going to annoy you a little bit, but it's probably not going to prevent you from driving yourself to your three jobs every day with the car you only *just* bought. Because what are you going to do about it? So it goes, you say. Now that you have a car, you're more or less stuck with it. Say the price of gas goes as high as $3.60, so that now, instead of spending $22.96 every week on gas, you're spending $25.27. That's $109.50 per month, $1,314.04 a year. Which reduces your monthly spending and saving money to about $940.

And as long as we are speaking hypothetically, a question which has often interested me is that of the price threshold at which car owners should actually consider the act of driving no longer worth the expense. I have heard all kinds of talk from drivers that I know about how if the price of gas goes up another cent it will be the end of driving. And I have seen the price of gas go up and have heard the threshold rise accordingly. I would like to see, just as an experiment, whether, if the national flat-rate of gasoline was five whole dollars, whether anybody would actually cease entirely to drive, and whether if it was ten dollars, there would be a considerable decrease in car and truck-traffic upon our roads. My hypothesis is that, very probably, it would not. And my guess is that we will not cease to buy and burn gasoline, at whatever the price, until it is no longer an available resource on our great mother Earth—or until there is a better way to make cars go.

We also have to consider the added financial responsibilities that are involved in owning a car. Car Insurance regulations vary from state to state, but most require that you have some sort of liability insurance for bodily injury and property damage. The national average cost for one year of auto insurance premiums in 2010 for males and females ages 18-25 was $1,566[2]. Translated to a monthly rate, that's roughly $130.50 per month. Which, assuming you're an average driver, reduces your monthly spending and savings money to about $809.50.

But that's not all. It probably also ought to be mentioned here how owning a car may going to lend you to inventing all kinds of excuses for driving it. Because when you have a car it makes life much easier to simply use it rather than *not* to use it. It's going to save you time, you think, which is, according to the same logic, going to save you money, also. So you're probably eventually going to start driving it more frequently than you originally intended. On the weekends it will give you a reason and a means to get out of town, to

_____

2 http://www.carinsurance.com. 22 May 2012.

take vacations, to visit old friends. You will drive two hundred miles just to make the most of your free time. On your off days you will call people and you will pick them up and go out to lunch. This will reduce your monthly spending and savings money to something like $750.00—but who's counting? This is still a good amount of money by itself, never mind the fact that you make nearly double that. You can live with the expense. Your movement base will grow. Your mobility will increase a thousand fold. You will become accustomed to long drives with your foot on the accelerator. The increased use of your car will cause considerable wear upon certain fan belts. You will become overdue for an oil-change and the knowledge of this will wear on you. On a particularly frosty morning you will start your car and wait for the defroster to defrost your windshield, and nothing will happen. You will take your car into the shop and will be told all at once of a thousand problems you have neglected. You will be told what it will cost to fix them and you will wonder how you will possibly be able to afford it, but you will pay it anyway and feel somehow that you have been overcharged for something, taken advantage of, perhaps, but you will also be powerless to argue the point. On some evening you may park your car and forget to turn your lights off, resulting in a dead battery. You will ask a stranger for help and he will help you, but the experience will be so unpleasant that you will invest in jumper cables, a car jack, and a spare tire, just for the hell of it. None of these are purchases you had planned on, and even though they are one-time expenses, as you imagine all of your car-repairs are, they will still cost you dearly. You may get careless behind the wheel and acquire several speeding tickets for exorbitant and unfair prices. You will spend all of a Saturday morning at the DA's office to argue your case before an indifferent judge, and will still have to pay. Eventually it will get so bad your insurance will increase, which will further reduce your available monthly saving and spending money. You will resolve to drive less, but will find yourself breaking that promise frequently. Your punctuality will drop off as you begin to spend more time in searching of parking. You will take risks for convenience sake, will acquire more tickets. You will lose sleep over the absurdity of your situation: that in a town of hundreds of thousands, there should be no place to go without taking your car, and nowhere to park once you've arrived. Perhaps driving home rather late one night you will hit a deer and will have to replace a headlight, or a fender, which will also cost you. You will find that you have been spending an awful lot of time at the auto-shop and have even read through all of their waiting-room literature, several times. You will wonder about how much time you have actually saved owning a car, and how much money it has actually allowed you to make. You will receive a bill for $899.99 and, without thinking, just so you can have your car back, you will sign for it. You will be told that your car is not in the best shape, that "she's an old girl, hasn't had a lot of road time, but doesn't seem to be made for the kind of miles she's been through." As a rule you will disregard advice from anybody who uses the feminine singular pronoun to refer to a machine. Your muffler may go, and you may receive a ticket for not getting it fixed right away. In time you will fix it and it will be more than you ever thought you would have to pay, but you will do it, counting it as a necessity, thinking that when the muffler's fixed, the car will be good-as-brand-new. You may be rear-ended unexpectedly one day on your way to work, and even if it was not your fault you may still have to pay a considerable sum to have your car repaired. If it is totaled you will be reimbursed, but for not nearly enough that you poured into that old hunks you loved. Who knows? Maybe when your car is totaled and you are back at square one, up to your knees in debt, you will think back on the whole experience of owning a car and you will say to yourself, "I think I would rather ride a bike than try that again." Then again, maybe all of this will affect you as no more than a slight annoyance, something troubling, maybe, but altogether bearable for the compensation of getting places "faster" and "saving time". So much depends upon the person and the kinds of chances they receive. But it ought to be kept in mind that truly anything is possible.

The point I'm trying to make here in saying all of this is that it's really not cheap or easy to own a car. It's an awful lot of responsibility, it's expensive, and it will give you something to worry about, if you don't have enough to worry about already. Based on the above example, choosing to ride a bicycle over a car could save you $1,200 a year on gasoline alone. Throw in some of the other expenses we've mentioned, along with the car itself, we're talking anywhere between $2,000 and $8,000 a year you could save. If you own a car, you already know what I'm talking about. If you don't own a car, but have unfettered access to one and are blessed with the privilege of driving it, it would probably benefit you to enroll in a car-mechanics class at the local Vocational Technical Institute as soon as possible so that the minute things begin to go wrong (as I promise, eventually, they will) you will know, first of all, whether they need to be fixed, how much it ought to cost to fix them, and maybe even how to do it yourself. It is but another of the many advantages to bicycling that the great majority of repairs and adjustments involved in owning and maintaining a bicycle do not require a highly specialized knowledge, or an exorbitant amount of money— at least in a relative, or say, comparative sense. A lot of bike mechanics is sheer practical common sense. Granted, there are things to learn: a certain amount of practice is required in order to develop the confidence, balance and skill-set necessary to be able to even *ride* a bike with any amount of success, much less to take one apart and put one back together. But a bicycle keeps few secrets.

5. There are no moral and/ or metaphysical reasons for why, given the option, I ought to choose a bicycle over a car.

Tell me, reader: is it not a little strange that in our cars and vans and trucks and busses, the engines are kept well-concealed beneath a hood? Why is this, do you suppose? Is a car really built so like a human being that it should be considered an act of public indecency to view it without all of its appropriate coverings? Who decides what are the appropriate coverings for an automobile? Who decides what are the appropriate coverings for a human being, for that matter? I was once privy to a rather heated argument between a police officer and the driver of a vehicle whose hood, for whatever reason, was missing from its hinges. The officer, so far as I could discern from my position at a nearby remove, was attempting to write the man a ticket for a traffic violation which the man refused to admit having committed. The officer threatened him and the man finally acquiesced to take his scolding, lest any further resistance any more perturb his judge, after which time the officer mentioned that the man ought to show a little more respect for his superiors, and that, by the way, he looked "ridiculous" driving around that way, and ought to feel ashamed to be seen in a car without a hood.

Respect? though I. Ridiculous? Ashamed? Is the hood of a car a symbol of power in this world—a kind of lion's roar or buck's antlers by which we in the wild jungle of the modern American city measure our worth and standing against one another? Does a hood represent the degree of our authority or our social status? Is it a consequence of our class? Perhaps it is to serve some far more practical function that our cars must keep their hoods. To keep the weather out, perhaps? I have heard it said that in some cases an overheated engine may have been easily prevented had the hood only been left open. And who can say what would or would not have prevented an overheated engine? Not driving at all might have just as well have prevented it. Perhaps it is to keep the engine in, then, that we must build our cars with hoods? But then it is certainly not true that a car will lose its engine if the hood is simply removed—no, this does not seem to be the answer, either. What then? What do gas-powered vehicles have to hide from us?

My educated guess is that it is primarily for aesthetic reasons that our cars are ever the better suited to conceal their engines beneath polished and painted hoods. The very first cars had no need for hoods—they were in fact so beset with problems requiring an engine-side inspection, it was all one could manage to try to keep his or her seat long enough to make any progress on a trip to town. A hood is a relatively recent development in the grand history of the functioning automobile, and was originally a kind of obstacle between a problem with the engine and its immediate solution. In fact, this is still the case. But I would be willing to bet that the constant sight of an automobile engine would be the cause for considerable discomfort, if not outright alarm, to some of us—akin, perhaps, to the way we might feel to see a doctor performing an open-heart surgery in broad daylight beneath the street-signs on the corner of Main and Broad. It's disgusting! people would say. How base! How rude! Mothers would probably seize their children to cover their eyes. Respectable pedestrians would simply turn around and begin walking in the other direction. Unfathomable!— Yet would it not give us a better idea into how our automobiles work, to be privy at all times to their engines? Would it not make us more conscious of the fact that what we are driving around in all day long are not merely four-wheeled recliners with radio and air-conditioning units—that, taken in another sense, our vehicles are extremely powerful, complicated machines, made of extremely durable, heavy, metal framing, beset with a complicated infrastructure of tubes and pipes and valves and monitors, the every wire of which serves some ultimate purpose in the grand design, the inner workings of which the large majority of us barely understand? Would we not be generally *more* wary of our proximity to other vehicles upon the road provided we only had some more insight into what a mess of pistons and connectors lay beneath the smooth underhoodings of our cars?

It remains to be seen whether making the engines of our vehicles perfectly transparent should result in an increased awareness of our responsibility that is inseparable from our power upon the road. Perhaps, at the very least, such transparency might serve to make us more interested in what we are doing whenever we are going anywhere by way of a synthetic engine. I am acquainted with certain people who, though they have been drivers all their lives, have never looked under the hood of their car and do not even know how to release the catch that would allow them to do so. "What's the difference whether I look or not?" they say. "I've come this far without ever needing to look—why should I need to now? There's a profession that exists for that. It doesn't happen to be mine." What audacity—this kind of reasoning! What complacence! What ignorance! There is a lot to cars that is better left under the hood; there is a lot to human beings that is better left under it, as well. But the engine—that is, how the machine actually works—I do not consider to be one of them.

I do not know whether my reader is very much like me or not, but I wish to know how all things work, how all things are made, the processes by which all things are reasoned and schemed and conceived, drafted and tried-out, bought and sold and exchanged and recombined and rebought and resold and finally thrown away or disposed of. I am preoccupied with narratives. Of all the unreasonable desires by which we are ever motivated or discouraged from any enterprise within this life, that which has always struck me as the least unreasonable is the desire to know the reasons for things. Beyond this, I do not think it should be entirely unreasonable of me to suggest that everybody ought to be like me in this one essential respect: we ought to do what we can to take and preserve an interest in ourselves, in our surroundings, and in all the life with which we must share these confined and temporary living-quarters of this beautiful, mewling terraqueous globe. If a reason must be provided for this, say that the primary good of struggling to remain interested in all of these things should consist in the degree to which such an endeavor should at least prevent us from *losing interest* in them, at which point, who can say what consequences should result?

But I suppose, being entirely realistic, even my own convictions—along with several observations touching upon our common humanity—will permit me to follow this blurted ethic only up to a point. The brevity of human life, for instance, will immediately present itself as a constraint to us in this fight never to lose our interest in the course of our living; as will our limited endurance, our need for sleep, the human tendency to change one's mind in spite of oneself—not to mention one's inevitable proneness to distraction, from which no individual is completely immune. It is a practical impossibility that one should ever attain equilibrium of interest touching all things; it is no less of an impossibility that anyone should ever wish to. In fact, the constant maintenance of equilibrium of interest in all subjects is one way of articulating the entire problem: the juxtaposition of headlines in the morning paper suggests that we ought to be as interested in what kind of dog the president is getting as with the rising mortality rates of the nation's homeless. A little priority from time to time would not hurt anybody.

Such observations as these behoove me to wonder whether there is, or whether there ought to be, a definite threshold beyond which my interest in a particular subject completely flounders, by necessity, when I grow entirely bored of the object I have taken under my sights, and must become exhausted, even insulted, by the sheer triviality of the labor of a thing's examination. We ought not to lose interest in our fellow human beings to the extent that we will knowingly allow them to suffer and die beneath a machinery which we may so easily write off as existing for our protection. Insofar as this threshold of what we are actually capable of being interested in, and the extent to which our interests are ever sustained at the expense of our interest in one another and ourselves, lie perhaps at the very heart of what I mean to be getting at in this essay, as well as in this life, let me see if I cannot identify for the reader, as precisely as I can, the location of that threshold—at least, as it sits with me, personally.

In the present case: underlying the hood of a car is a mechanism the workings of which, I am not ashamed to admit, I possess little-to-no understanding. My history as a student of the world teaches me that there is an explanation that would allow me to understand the contraption—one physical, one chemical, one mechanical, one electrical. Perhaps others may be found as well, each of which would partially explain the transferences and energy-exchange processes which are constantly taking place behind the ignition key and the foot-treadles of the gas and break. Of course I know that I am free to take the time to study these processes: however, to drive the vehicle, I am certainly not required to know how many cylinders my engine contains, nor even where the gas tank is located. To receive my driver's license (in the state of Pennsylvania, in September of 2004), I was only required only to make sure that my passenger's seat-belt was fastened like my own, that my three mirrors allowed me to see properly behind me, and that I was able to use my turn-signal. That is not to say it could give me no advantage as a user of the roadway to be better acquainted with the names of all the parts of my car, to own a car-mechanic's mind and instinct, as well as a portable tool kit in the trunk for any and every possible problem that may potentially arise. On the contrary—I should think that all of these things definitely *would* be of some benefit to me, if not as a cautious and skillful driver, than at least as curious individual who considers himself for the most part interested in what he is about, whenever he is about it. But I say again: so much is not required in the least.

The criticism has been made of the generation of twenty-somethings in this country, (born sometime between the end of the nineteen-eighties and the start of the nineties), that with all the innovations in media, technology, and communications that have been introduced to the world within our lifetime, we have begun to experience a faster, easier, more connected world and worldview, far surpassing anything our preceding generation could have imagined in the days of their youth— and that this easier way of being has come to us at the definite expense of something. This criticism is by no means a new one. It is the same criticism our grandparents delivered to our parents when they were our age—it is probably the same one we shall be telling our children: You do not know how good you have it—you do not know how hard it used to be. But of course it is even older than that. Every successive generation has been vastly different from the one that came before, and still every generation has passed into the next, without hope of gaining immortality for itself. History, meanwhile, has been teaching all along that there is no time like the present. This familiar criticism of the younger generation by the old is predicated on the assumption that the future holds some sort of trajectory of improvement in store for us, and that this progression is towards a Goodness. It understands history to be a movement towards a better world, and is hopelessly, tragically optimistic.

There is a difference, of course, in the referents every critic applies to every age. No two successive generations are, or have been exactly the same. What was once considered progress in the mode of transportation that led one from being the passenger of a train to the driver of an automobile was afterwards considered in the mode of writing that led from being author of the handwritten manuscript to author of a typewritten one. Each of these progressions came out of different periods of time, in different modes of consumption, wherein the consumer was forced to redefine him- or herself (happily, or begrudgingly) around the introduction of a new apparatus onto a universal market. "It will change your life," the consumer was told. "And change is good." Or: "It will change history." And that doesn't mean the future. To such changes, there are always those who have resisted, who have clung to their way of doing things, having no need for anything more or any better than what is. In time, however, these leave-behinds come to seem as the outcasts of their age—curmudgeons, wily and stubborn bandicoots. Progress runs on in spite of them, and leaves them quite behind.

But what is the "something" that is expended in the name of progress? When an inferior technology is outmoded by a superior one that will perform the same task in less time, for less money, with less labor—what is lost, merely, but the simple inferiority of the old way of doing things? I would like to offer here (without quoting Marx or any of his intellectual offspring) that one of the possible answers to this question is our own ability to give substantial and adequate account for ourselves—not only in a historical sense, but more importantly, in either a fictional, spontaneous, mythical or religious one, as well. It is no coincidence that a computer's storage space is referred to as its Memory. The faster we make the minds and memories of our artificial intelligences, the greater risk we run of losing, even more than the capacity for maintaining our own, the very desire and *need* for any living, present, human memory.

That we are a culture already dispossessed of its myths does not need to be shown. That we are becoming a culture disposed of its memory remains to be acknowledged. In his 1991 book *The Cry for Myth*, Rollo May draws a direct connection between the problems of a post-modern American society and the absence of any culturally relevant narrative frame of reference:

The fact that Western society has all but lost its myths was the main reason for the birth and development of psychoanalysis in the first place...Many of the problems of our society, including cults and drug addiction, can be traced to the lack of myths which will give us as individuals the inner security we need in order to live adequately in our day. The sharp increase in suicide among young people and the surprising increase in depression among people of all ages are due...to the confusion and the unavailability of adequate myths in modern society[3].

Nietzche made the same claim of German society in 1887.

We have approximated the same conditions ever since the Alexandrian-Roman revival in the fifteenth century, after the long entr'acte so difficult to describe. Today we experience the same extravagant thirst for knowledge, the same insatiable curiosity, the same drastic secularization, the nomadic wandering, the greedy rush to alien tables, the frivolous apotheosis of the present or the stupefied negation of it...like symptoms pointing to a comparable lack in our own culture, which has also destroyed myth[4].

But what does it mean to belong to a society that has lost or "destroyed" its myths? One of the primary original functions of myths was to provide

---

3 May, Rollo. *The Cry For Myth. Pp 9.*
4 Nietzsche, Friedrich. *The Birth of Tragedy.* Pp 139-140.

humanity with some basis for understanding
not only the origins of its own unfathomable
existence, but also the reasons for why things
happened which otherwise eluded the human
capacity for explanation. It is to be imagined that
in the beginning, whenever curious humankind
stumbled upon any phenomenon for which it
could not account, the best thing to do was to
try to draft a story to explain it. We may assume
that this happened by instinct. In the primordial
fog that lingered at the crossroads of the rational
and the imaginable began the realm of myth. At
some indefinable juncture in human history began
the creation of the vast catalogue of the dramatis
personae of the universe. The phenomenon even
of the echo—now known by the provable laws of
physics to be nothing other than the mere reaction
of a sound-wave thrown at a quantifiable decibel
and direction against the edges of confinement
whose measurable convexity or concavity may be
called the sole determinant of the efficacy of any
call's response—was once to be comprehended only
through a story: Hera had condemned Echo "never
to use her tongue again, except to repeat what was
said to her"[5]. This was no exercise of divine justice:
divine whim, rather, had brought the condition of
eternity down upon her. It only suited Hera best

---

5 Hamilton, Edith. *Greek Mythology.* Pp. 87.

to punish Echo when Zeus's whereabouts and infidelities could not be discovered—not because Echo was the guilty party, but because she was fair, and, as circumstance would have it, nearby to Hera's wrath. Her only crime in being the most beautiful of woodland nymphs to ever love the unlovable Narcissus had been in announcing it within range of Hera's hearing.

And yet here, in the whimsy of the gods, is what we must admire in the pagan myths. The genius of Greek mythology consisted in the fact that all of its personages, save only in their capacity to live without ever suffering to die, were otherwise, in every respect, human. The best explanations that myths could provide to satisfy the absurd "desire of reason"—that is, the hunger of a mortal humankind to know something, anything, for certain—were themselves consistent upon the irrational actions and behaviors of the immortals, whose only advantage over humankind—that they could not die—was also, in a manner of speaking, also their greatest disadvantage. Out of the decrees, mandates, and the blundering injustice of the gods, came, piecemeal, every worldly wonder. Hence, the mulberry is "the everlasting memorial" of Pyramus and Thisbe; the linden and the oak tree grow together because Baucis loved and was loved by Philemon; the familiar Hyacinth bears its name not for the botanist who discovered it but, *in memoriam*, for Apollo's dearest friend who was accidently slain in a discus competition with the deathless god. It should be said that the myths never completely succeeded in providing the Greeks with the rational explanations out of which the need for their existence as narratives originally sprang. But then this was never their intended purpose. Their usefulness was in their provision of a frame of reference whereby the gods and their behavior would not be discounted by humankind as unfamiliar or incomprehensible. As Nietzsche puts it: "The gods justified human life by living it themselves—the only satisfactory theodicy ever invented"[6].

But this reconstruction is only the account of what has been lost. That Golden Age of European Reason, formally known as The Enlightenment, was the death blow to our capacity for the creation or the entertainment of myth. The rational ability to explain had extended itself by way of the scientific method so far into that foggy atmosphere congregated at the crossroads where a speculative and perspicacious religion had been the mainstay, it eventually found itself emerging in some considerable clarity on the other side, with little, if anything left at which to wonder, and no way merely

6 Nietzsche, Friedrich. *The Birth of Tragedy. Pp. 30.*

to return. What has been brought to our attention lately, within this generation, is that the innovations in our technologies are not actually innovations at all, but are merely complications of the issue, variations upon a theme. What contemporary markets have learned to buy and sell is the concept of innovation without changing the product or its function. That "this will do what nothing has done before" is the oldest trick in the book—but it remains one for which the consumer has not ceased to fall.

A correlation presents itself here between the rapid flourishing development of new technologies—upon which we are becoming increasingly dependent, in spite of knowing less and less about how they work—and our diminishing capacity and desire to create meaningful, *imaginative* narratives to provide sufficient account for ourselves. Myths are no longer accredited as worth believing in. Their importance has been confined to the realm of history, which itself does not bear very much upon reality anymore. We no longer know how to "carry on" having only our stories to stand in where our explanations falter. Science must now do what myths once only ever tried—to provide us with the Truth. All the rest we consider make-believe.

But science is also pushing us further from our own understanding of our surroundings, with the increased specialization that should be required to understand how things work. The truth is, the latest model of cellular telephone that appears in the shopfront window will do what every cellular telephone has done before it. It will only do them faster, and within the confines of a smaller, more portable device. This correspondence of an increased function within a diminishing size yields the consumer the freedom to carry less. You will considerably reduce your suffering with this product, the commercial goes, in so many words. Which leads us to another perspective of history: The same innovations which have supposedly made faster and easier the means by which we are able to keep in touch, communicate, access information, travel, consume, know, understand, read, talk, write, and experience the world, generally, have also, themselves, become not only more difficult to understand, but harder to care about understanding. The number of us who actually understand how the Internet works is in the excessive minority to those of us whose only concern is with the fact that it does. We are increasingly alienated not only from what we are buying and operating, but from knowing how the things operate beneath our wills, and hands, and eyes, and most importantly, *our interests*.

Should you ever ask anybody to explain why

or what exactly it is they do not understand about something which you have been telling them, which they have just told you they do not understand, it seems to me that either one of two things may occur. Either they will tell you a little more about it than they have let on, and show you that they actually do understand, if only a little; that what they are calling a "lack of understanding" is really only a lack of depth of understanding mixed with a habit of speaking in absolutes—or they will end the conversation by reiterating the fact, by looking at you and stuttering something while maybe a sliver of drool slips out of the side of their mouth. I suppose I do not understand the internet because I simply do not understand the internet. But I would like to qualify my understanding, or my lack thereof, in this case, by saying this: that the reason I do not understand the internet is not the same reason I do not understand advanced calculus, thermodynamics, how a carburetor works, or *Finnegan's Wake*. These are all things I do not understand, quite simply, because I have not really made much of an effort towards understanding them. The way I do not understand the internet is more closely affiliated with the way I do not understand how it can be that the average American spends six hours a day watching television—which is to say: I don't understand how this passive activity has got so many of us by the throat, or why it should be so hard to shake.

The way the bicycle fits into this discussion is in its optimality as comprehensible technology that is not in any danger of disappearing as a legitimate means of travel, that has the potential to ground us once more in the fog of wonder where our imaginations may once more flourish into making meaningful narratives. The way the bicycle does this is by exposing its rider more directly to the world. When one travels by bicycle, one has a better sense of the landscape through which he or she has travelled when he or she arrives. One is reacquainted with one's surroundings—with the weather and the land, with the shape of the road. One remembers the hills of a journey in the pain and soreness of one's muscles following the arrival, in the wind that lingers in one's hair. One thinks more of the trees when one can only escape their looming shadows by one's own means. One is more open to conversing with strangers of all kinds upon a bicycle because one is not hidden behind a virtually sound-proof glass. One is more available to help those who are in need of it, and I would even argue, more *willing* to help a fallen traveler than automobilists, though they are often equipped with less. Riding a bicycle breeds a concern for others the same way driving a car diminishes the same inclination, and may even develop the converse.

I for one am feeling the reverse effects of this so called "progression" towards the easier life. I am compelled, for whatever reason, to resist the use of any mechanism whose function, independent of my operation of it, eludes my understanding. It is for this reason that I will not condemn all drivers of all automobiles. An automobile, I recognize, is a means of transportation that exists as a legitimate means of travel, that is useful, and that consists mainly of processes which it should not be impossible to understand. It is for this reason (among several others) that I myself do not drive a gas-powered vehicle: I do not currently possess the knowledge of every piece of any vehicle's engine, nor the interest sufficient to learning every piece of it. For myself, I should count this latter insufficiency as the base criteria for my own (and anybody's) use and operation of any vehicle: *If I could not build it myself, I ought not to be driving it.* For I desire to move only by that means which I can fully comprehend. For this reason I must rule out, for the time being, all flying aircrafts, gas or battery powered machines, trains, subways, trolleys, ocean steamers, ferries, vans, mopeds, go-carts, and motorcycles. The mechanics of my bicycle are enough to occupy my mechanical attentions for the present.

And what unfathomable desire is it, my dear reader, which yields us to the complaint simply to further understand? Insufficiency of knowledge is always a cry born of suffering. It is terrible to me not to know how things work—almost as terrible as it is to me to consider how little interest my fellow human beings seem to take in their means of motion, and so often in each other. We *all* ought to take more of an interest in how we move around. I will make the suggestion here that if we will insist upon taking an airplane anywhere, we ought at least to be asking for blueprints into the construction of the plane itself, hard and comprehensive materials for studying how a jet engine actually operates—rather than a pillow, a cocktail, and a pair of headphones, the better to enjoy the in-flight movie with the hopes of being coaxed into unconsciousness. Life is a short enough trip already—one for whose inestimable duration it is already difficult enough to remain awake without being pampered into submission. My only request in trying is that I not be passengerized whilst airborn to the point that I am docile on the ground, nor asked to pay money that I earned in my fixed workplace so that I should not have to feel the miles or see the expansive ranges my traveling moves me through. It is best that we should know how far a mile is *in our legs,* that we may also know how much there is worth exploring in it. With a mile for our reference, I do believe we would the better appreciate a journey of three thousand, or three hundred thousand.

6. The bicycle is far more difficult to comprehend than the automobile, and can yield me no better understanding of myself in riding it.

Come, now! But this is simply not true, reader! Neither the bicycle nor the automobile may qualify as a simple machine, but it is a fact that the bicycle is a *simpler* machine than the gas-powered automobile. I cannot pretend to explain to you the process by which gasoline is converted into momentum. I could perhaps refer you to several books on the subject which I have tried examining for myself, but I cannot recommend them, as taken altogether they amount to little else to me but a puzzling literature written in a jargon that is well-nigh impossible to decipher short of becoming a mechanic's apprentice.

But take my bicycle: Here. Observe it. Notice how all its mechanisms—with the exception, maybe, of the stem, the bottom bracket, and certain portions of the wheel—are worn upon its sleeves? You may turn a bicycle upon its shoulders and, merely by turning the crank arm and keeping close watch of the chain clenched in the teeth about the cogs of the rear wheel's cassette, perceive all the essential physics that are involved in making a bicycle go. You may squeeze the break with your hand and perceive the tensing of the break-cable that is the means by which it stops. The bicycle is a kind of mountable crustacean in this regard, insofar as its anatomy is worn as the exoskeleton.

Beyond this, the bicycle does not divorce the individual from a greater knowledge of him- or herself. In fact, it encourages a curiosity of the bicyclist's own living organism. If anyone will try to get at what *really* makes a bicycle go, one would have to perform a surgery and take apart the human legs, study the calf muscles and the hams that may be found there, as well as their unique adherence to the bones, follow the nerve- and artery chords which may be discovered among their sinews as the signal- and oxygen- and hormone-carriers, all the way up the spinal column to the separate command-centers of the headquarter brain and heart, humankind's equally-ranked, antagonistic commodores, and confront that great wide mystery of life that originates and terminates but inevitably eludes us there.

Even our language accounts for the difference in the kind of adventure and enjoyment it should be possible to derive from the bicycle versus the car. We do not *ride* our cars—we ride *in* them. When we must go somewhere in our cars, we *drive* them. The English word "automobile" is derived from the Greek "auto," meaning "self" and the Latin "mobilis," meaning "movable." By whatever logic this word was originally assigned to represent the automobile we know today, to think of it as a machine that "drives itself" would be fallacious. The English language has done its best to distinguish the passenger from the driver of a gas-powered vehicle, so that it is practically impossible, in a linguistic sense, to enjoy the benefits of the passenger of an automobile while suffering to be its driver, and vice versa. The driver of a vehicle cannot surrender his attention from the immediate task of driving the car any more than the passenger, however annoyed by the driver's driving, cannot simply take control of the vehicle, short of seizing the wheel by violence. These roles are separate in vehicles by the assignments of our seats. But *to ride* a bike: think of it! Is there any other mechanism built for individual transportation under the sun that may at once yield an individual to such a strong impression of his own agency in his traveling, even as it may let him feel that he is completely wanting of the same faculty? Even upon a live horse, the rider is at the mercy of the stamina and consciousness of the horse itself: if the horse falls, so too falls the rider riding it, with all the blame for the stumble to befall the speechless animal. Upon a bicycle, however, though the individual may pedal and steer and drive herself where and how she may, even as she pedals, she is in no small way a passenger, too. The bicyclist is a passenger even as she is the driver—at once master and slave of her own wandering destiny.

7. *Bicycling is much less convenient than a car.*

Bicycling much less convenient than a car?! Phooey, I say, to that. What could be more convenient than using your own legs to power yourself? What could be more convenient than a vehicle that does not depend upon any ulterior source of fuel but the rider's energy to function? Does state law stipulate that a bicyclist must have a license to ride a bicycle? Of course not! Does it stipulate that one must have insurance to ride a bicycle? No. Must the bicyclist wait for endless hours at the Department of Motor Vehicles—for any reason, ever? No. When a road is closed for a fallen tree, does the traffic cop deny the bicyclist entrance? He doesn't. When the bicyclist arrives at the theater-house with only a moment to spare, does he or she spend the first act of the play searching for a place to park? No. During the intermission, must the bicyclist leave his or her company of friends again to walk a block to pay a meter? No. And when the show is over, does the bicyclist have an officer's ticket for seventy-five dollars discreetly left on his or her bicycle for parking in front of a fire-hydrant? No. When the bicyclist's bike breaks down on the roadside, is he or she so stranded that a tow-truck must come and hall away his or her bike for an exorbitant fee? No. When a bicyclist's bike breaks down is he or she completely helpless and afraid for the lack of knowledge of what could potentially be wrong? No. In winter, must the bicyclist wait half-an-hour for his or her windshield to defrost before he or she can leave his or her driveway? No. When there is a snowstorm, must the bicyclist spend all of a Sabbath morning digging his or her bicycle out of the mountain of snow beneath which the plows have buried it? No. In the springtime, when the flowers bloom, is the bicyclist prevented from stopping to smell the honeysuckle on the roadside for lack of anywhere to park? No. Is the bicyclist ever beset with a dead battery? No. Must the bicyclist frequently visit the local garage to have his or her windshield wipers replaced? No. Must the bicyclist change his or her motor oil? No. Must the bicyclist replace his or her muffler? She musn't. Will a bicycle be damaged in a hailstorm? No. Is the bicyclist ever given a ticket for speeding? No. When a car alarm goes off in a quiet neighborhood, is it ever the bicyclist who is the recipient of angry calls from the neighbors? It isn't. What, then, has the car to do with *convenience?* I say that a car is one of the least convenient contraptions ever invented, and much less convenient than a bicycle, too.

8. *Bicycling requires far more maintenance than a car.*

I am afraid this is like splitting hairs, reader! Compared to the numerous malfunctions to which a gas-powered vehicle remains susceptible, I'm afraid one has no argument here. It is true a bicycle does require some maintenance—but this is true of everything one owns. The primary advantage to owning a bicycle over a car, with respects to the kinds of maintenance that you should ever be required to perform on it, is that if something is wrong with your bicycle, it will not wait to reveal itself to you until you are on the eve of your vacation—rather, it will speak the trouble to you instantly and directly. If your wheel is out-of-true, this should be easy enough to tell by how wobbly it feels to ride. If you break a spoke, you will be able to hear that you have broken it. If you get a puncture in your tube, you will feel your rim upon the street in your wrists upon the bars. If your chain lacks lube, you may hear it, or may feel it in your pedaling. If the bearings of your fork have rusted, you will know by what a grating thing it is to steer yourself in any direction. If your breaks are jammed you will have no freedom to accelerate. There is nothing automatic about a bicycle: this is to the owner's advantage.

Not so in a car. While we may consider it a very good argument "for our convenience" to consider all of the automated trinkets and processes which cars contain—radios, heating- and air-conditioning units, break-lights, windshield wipers, blinkers, power-windows, power-steering, electronic locks, speedometers, fuel gauges, and temperature gauges, to name but a few—the trouble with owning a great assortment of things that are *supposed to function by themselves* is that when they do not, the owner may be entirely at a loss to know either how to perform manually the tasks which the mechanism originally did, or how to repair the malfunction. Granted, this is not always the case, but I would argue that the more we rely upon what is automatic, the less automatic we become ourselves. It is a frustrating feeling that besets you to have to pull over the minute it starts raining and wait out the storm because you do not know how to fix your windshield wipers, and cannot fathom even so much as what might be wrong with them. Indeed—such a circumstance provides us with an example of something that is what I would call the exact *opposite* of convenient. That's annoying, we say. That's frustrating. Just like it's frustrating to have to walk home seven miles because your car broke down and while you were planning on being home in ten minutes, you now must admit to yourself that in reality it will be more like two and a half hours. That *is* annoying. It is a rather well known phenomenon, the way we do occasionally call our vehicles "worthless" and "junk" and "bastard" and "piece of shit" and other names when they do not do what they are supposed to do. Based on my personal experience and observation of my fellow humanity, it seems that to the extent that people are ever willing to personify their cars into objects deserving of those feelings with which we are in the habit of reserving for the various abstractions we hold of one another, hate is far more commonly hurled upon the automobile one drives than love. When a car is functioning as it is supposed to, it is little else than a machine which is serving its purpose as a means to an end. Either it is useful in getting us quickly where we need to go, or it is at fault—lazy—a thing worth hating because to love it would be simply impossible.

I do not know if it would be considered a wise ethic to try treating a machine only as we should like to be treated, but I personally do not see the sense in allowing oneself to become so upset at a body of metal which can in no way respond to anything that you can think (or feel) to say to it, that can ultimately take no responsibility for its malfunctioning. No— this is something which only people can do, which many of us prefer *not* to do because to do that, to actually take responsibility for the knowledge of the way things work which we say *ought to be automatic* should seriously diminish the extent to which we should derive any sort of enjoyment from the mechanism as an object that exists to make our lives easier. To take responsibility for something whose entire existence is literally dripping with the notion of *"so you don't have to"* should strike us as seriously contradictory—and does. "No," one says to this. "I will not. I will not learn how to change the oil; I will not learn how to check the fluids; I will not learn how to wire a lightbulb. I will not do these things because I paid good money so that I shouldn't have to." One's convenience is hindered the moment responsibility for an object is transferred back onto the driver.

But I'm just going to go ahead and say here that we ought to; we ought to take a little responsibility for those things around us that we like to think of as being completely "other" to us, the things which we say possess a function and even an intelligence that is entirely separate to our own. We ought to take responsibility for what is automatic in the world, for what we have made, for what we buy and sell and dispense with, if only so that we may not forget that none of it has really been necessary. We may better develop our enjoyment of the conveniences surrounding us in our contemporary American society by becoming used to the idea of doing without a few of them. I will be the first to call myself a dreamer: but it has been a dream of mine that I should some day hear the conversion story of the automobilist who, pulling over in a rainstorm to ask the uncovered pedestrian whether he would like a lift, or at least a little shelter, is not only declined his offering, but is, in turn, actually invited to walk for several miles in the rain with the pedestrian, and, having neither the sort of character that would give him to laughing in a foreigner's face, nor the sort of fear which we are taught as children to breed for strangers, nor the sort of attachments to his worldly possessions which would prevent him from abandoning them without a thought at a moment's notice, agrees, simply, and gets out and walks, companioned, the rest of his days, never looking back.

The danger in becoming angered by our cars translates to the dangerous attitudes it breeds in becoming upset at other people for things that actually are out of their control. When something that is automatic malfunctions, it has the potential to make the owner of so many automatic processes feel his or her ignorance in a way that is almost insulting. This is an unhealthy kind of anger, reader—to become upset at something because it has worn down, or broken, without ever having assured you of its own volition that it couldn't or wouldn't. If driving a car is going to make you so upset, I would recommend not driving any more.

As far as bicycle maintenance goes, a good rule for knowing how or what to maintain on your bicycle would be to consider your bicycle along with yourself. If you come in from a ride completely covered in mud and think it would be a good idea to take a shower— consider your bicycle, as well, which was also on that ride, which may also be as filthy as you. Don't you think it would be nice to give your bicycle a good scrubbing, in addition to yourself? If you do, you should probably just do it. Granted, you will have no reward for this. Your bicycle will not hug you or kiss you or say thank you. But maintenance is not really about being rewarded. It's about preventing what might potentially turn into an inconvenient situation. If you maintain your bicycle and its parts, you may have to replace parts less frequently, may get more use out of your bicycle, and may come to learn how to maintain a bicycle even faster in the future.

9. *Bicycling is dangerous.*

This is certainly true. But then so is driving a car. The decision to make any kind of motion in this world at all makes for a kind of inevitable perilousness. Come to think of it, so does the decision not to. There is something extremely dangerous about the decision even to stay home and work on one's knitting in the company of the family cat. To live in the world and be at the same time out of harm's way is a contradiction in terms— for this is a world of contrasts. I am certainly open to imagining others—worlds wherein one's desires and interests are as constant and provable as simple mathematics, where it is not possible to suffer or die, a world where, for that reason, the stakes of life should be pretty low; but I cannot ignore that the factualness of such a world is only in reference to this world as its imagined opposite—i.e., in contrast. Such a world does not exist in itself, anywhere, any more than the quality of danger does. For when we speak of a thing's dangerousness, we are speaking of a thing in contrast with another, something that is better in reference to something worse, something that remains possible set against the reality one may be hoping for. To be merely *in danger* usually refers one to one's mortality. An endangered species is at the risk of extinction. When a man is wanted by the police, he is called "armed and dangerous" so that one will think that any encounter with him may leave one dead. The sign on a tractor's rototiller fender reads, merely: DANGER and depicts the silent cartoon of a man in a cautionary yellow world being drawn arm-first into the spinning blades of his demise, having been already gobbled past the elbow. The sign on any power station fence reads, similarly: DANGER: HIGH VOLTAGE and depicts a human hand scored by a lightning bolt. What dangers do these signs express but those which may snuff us out? What technique do they employ as the best means of raising our awareness of what it should be possible to suffer in this world but that of the worst possible outcome, brought to the fore in parody of a potential likeness? Probably there ought to be more of these signs, made for any and every situation, and posted everywhere until there were no other color in our sight but yellow. A cartoon of a car or a truck with the word DANGER underscoring it should perhaps be made and put up every half mile on every road in the country, that we may not forget what a danger is an automobile to our person. A cartoon of a human being, or better yet, of two human beings, standing side by side, should perhaps illustrate the greatest danger of all. I do not know if it would be more or less of a distraction to simply have a DANGER sign that was nothing but a mirror, but if this could somehow be achieved, it would drive the point home most directly: what we ought to be thinking about when we are in danger (and we are always in danger) is what we are doing, right now, this very mment, and what kind of harm it should be possible for us to cause ourselves or others in the event that the attention we are paying to what we are doing should, for even a moment, for whatever reason, lapse.

There is, or course, no evidence that the physical presence of WARNING and DANGER and CAUTION signs ever have or ever will prevent accidents from happening. Danger signs are present not wherever there is the possibility of human death, but wherever there is the possibility of a legal liability. One must take one's fault into one's own hands as soon as a sign is put up, the prosecution says. And the defense will unfailingly retort that such signs were not visible enough, or that they were not clear enough to prevent what happened from taking place. The logic here is that if only the signs had been clearer, a little bigger, maybe a little more threatening, perhaps someone who no longer is, would still be here today. Somebody else must be at fault when injuries occur, for it is simply unimaginable to us that one should or could put oneself in the way of a clear and present danger. But I say that it is imaginable, it is possible, that whoever enjoys the benefits of existing runs the risk, at every moment, of losing it all, and should try, as best one can, to keep that in mind. I say this not because it should decrease the surprise of accidents, or eliminate the shock from trauma, but because remaining vigilant is maybe the only thing that may decrease the probability of an accident's occurring in the first place. The trouble is that the human being is so expert an adapter that even if she is made aware of her death every time she turns a corner, she may become so used to the information and the means by which it is transmitted, that she may grow tired of hearing about it all the time, and may even cease to pay attention to it. In our accustomedness to being, it is neither impossible nor even very difficult that we should potentially lose sight of and even entirely forget that we are mortal. Having never died, it is easy to imagine that we never will. Having never given it much time or dwelling in our imagination, it is simple to think, without even realizing that we are thinking it, that we cannot.

But I realize this is itself a rather dangerous line of thinking. "What point is he driving at?" you must be wondering. Only this: that there is nothing in the world that may not be called dangerous—that that is hardly a reason *not* to do something, especially something as enjoyable and productive and as efficient and as conscientious as deciding to ride your bicycle instead of driving your car. Not to feel safe riding one's bicycle *because* of cars, and to make *that* your reason *for* driving is to overlook the right to the roadway which the bicyclist shares equally with the motorist. It is also to assign a false safety-value to being in a car, which one ought not to do. One may certainly *feel* safer in a car; but this is an illusion which being in cars allow people to feel without trying. In a car, one may move at seventy miles per hour and sip hot tea from a porcelain cup, all the while maintaining the illusion from the interior of the vehicle that one is not moving at all. One may also look out the window of a vehicle and regard a cyclist and imagine that he or she who is driving the vehicle occupies the safer of two means, perhaps without considering, for even a moment, that the driver of a vehicle is in greater danger of being the potential cause of harm to the cyclist than the cyclist is of causing harm to the driver of the vehicle.

It is to overlook life's other dangers, as well: that it is a dangerous thing, for instance, even to love other people. Ah—but if I had only one piece of advice for you, whoever you are, it would be to go and try to love someone. Even if you fail at it; even if you get hurt; even if it comes to seem the most dangerous thing of all. Keep trying. Because it is also impossible to be completely free from the possibility of causing harm to others—and it is love that makes this so. It is because of love that we hurt when our loved ones are hurt; because of love that we lose when the ones we love have been lost; because of love that even in the act of dying ourselves, we do not decrease the misery and suffering with which the living dwell, who loved us, however well it may relieve us of our own—that our own dying may only increase the suffering they must endure who are left to live without us. It is a dangerous thing to love, indeed; it is a dangerous thing to hate; it is a dangerous thing to be happy; just as it is dangerous to be unhappy. Provided the occasion is married with a miserable enough consequence to make you fearful of ever trying it again, there is nothing that will leave us free from danger. But it is for love that life's mysteries renew; for love that living keeps its beauty; for love that we keep trying.

So for chrissake wear a helmet and keep your eyes open, and try to be aware of what remains possible while you are out there enjoying what is unfolding perfectly according to plan.

10. *Bicycling has no health advantages.*

Bicycling has no health advantages?! Most of the people I see running around outdoors these days have the exercise for their excuse—as though they would rather you thought them concerned with their health and well-being, as opposed to being unconcerned with it entirely and merely outside, literally running around, because they had felt some uncontrollable compulsion to go and see all, as quickly as possible, or simply to see as much of what is going on in the world today, in one's immediate vicinity, as possible, and to be taken to it by the power of one's own willful energies. Yet consider how the exercise of bicycling may develop the quality of a pervasive interestedness, and what a healthy thing it is to be interested! Consider how bicycling as an exercise may reduce your cholesterol and your blood pressure, improve your circulation, and strengthen your heart—even while allowing you to get places you would be going anyway. Consider how devoting a little more time to a daily exercise could become a new and productive hobby for you to devote your spare time to, and may reduce the occasions you may have for feeling depressed. Consider the leg-strength bicycling may allow you to develop! Consider the weight you could lose! What is more—consider that by deciding to ride your bicycle, you are actually improving the quality of the earth's breathable air, not only for yourself, but for everyone, insofar as you are *not* driving an automobile. Consider how improving your own health could improve the health of people you are close to, and may inspire others to do the same. Consider how riding your bicycle with others may develop an acquaintanceship into a friendship, and may strengthen preexisting bonds thereof. In consideration of all this, finally, consider what an exercise in motionlessness it is to drive a car, what a bother it is to keep one's eyes open upon such long drives as one is wont to take, how strong is the desire when one is sitting still to move one's body somehow. And when all of this has been considered, then try and tell me that bicycling has no health advantages.

11. *Bicycling has no proven psychological advantages.*

No psychological advantages?! Consider how *good* it feels to ride your bike, reader, to arrive where you have intended to go with your own legs having brought you, having breathed the world's fresh air in the transit, having exercised, having paid nothing for gasoline, having improved your heart-rate, having made no extraneous stops, having avoided traffic jams, having had no trouble finding a place to park your vehicle, having provided yourself with more energy for your day, having arrived precisely where you intended to go by a means you fully understand and thoroughly enjoy. What could be more psychologically advantageous but the happy exhaustion with which you dismount your iron steed?

12. *Bicycling cannot improve my community.*

Improve your community?! Imagine for a moment a world without cars, a city like Venice, in which merely to enter, one must park one's vehicle outside the gates and walk to be admitted. Imagine parading a highway void of cars. Imagine a city whose noises were not composed of the sounds of rushing cars and trucks! Consider that more than 40,000 deaths occur in America each year owing to car-related injuries and accidents. Consider also that the amount of resources that could be saved if everyone were riding a bike would be absolutely staggering. Without want of gasoline, who knows what kinds of global disasters we might prevent? Wars might be avoided altogether if more people made a greater effort to quit driving. It has been shown that the energy and amount of raw material that is needed to manufacture a single automobile would translate roughly to the amount of material one would need to make a hundred bicycles. Consider the jobs that would be created if we were to suddenly start making bicycles in this country out of our cars! What is more, consider that entire communities have already formed around the practice of bicycling, that there are as many bicycle cooperatives in this country as there are major cities, that all roads in this country are connected to one another, that whenever we stand upon a street, we are literally on a paved pathway to anywhere and everything, that it's the entire world our bicycles give us access to, not merely the world we know...

—But that is enough arguing for now. While all of these reasons may be offered in resistance to driving, they will not entirely account for me and why it became so imperative for me to attempt crossing the country on my bicycle. Perhaps it should be said, here, as a kind of disclaimer to my audience—especially for the benefit of those among us who may have little or no inclination whatsoever towards cycling; who may be altogether ignorant of both the history of the bicycle as a mechanical innovation and a means of superior individual transportation, as well as its legacy as an instrument of human achievement; whose excitements, or otherwise curiosities, as a reader, in happening upon what I have so far managed to suggest regarding the journey that I attempted, were raised merely under the false pretense that I had been the first either to conceive of such an undertaking, or to execute it outright—there was nothing novel in the idea for the journey I had planned to take. Indeed, there is nothing new under the sun—but misconceptions still arise. I've honestly no idea who was the first person to ever cross the United States upon a bicycle. I've no idea if it was a man or a woman, if he or she was white or black or red or yellow; if he or she crossed north to south or east to west; if he or she did it merely to be first, or if there was something more like necessity in the motivation.

It hardly matters. To be first is, to my mind, the last reason I should ever like to try anything—for I count myself a member of the human race, not a leader of it; and so far as the potential of my experiences are concerned, I will admit, others have come before me, and others will come after. I only have, for my own part, a lot of catching up to do. The misconception I would here throw off, of having myself mistaken for a pioneering cyclist, is bound up, inseparably, I'm afraid, with being mistaken for some narrator from whom you have already heard. No, I am not the first to attempt the crossing of America upon two self-propellant wheels—it were more accurate to say I was, for a short while, only among that enormous population of the latest who had tried it. But neither should it be thought that it were only to the pioneer that we are best fitted as an audience. Quite the contrary. It seems to me it is precisely in the variation and in the deviation from the pioneer's successful course that we ought to try to understand. For every individual life, human and otherwise, is being lived, this very moment, its first and only time. We are all pioneers who dwell and roam upon this globe. Suffice it then to say, my journey was a pioneer's, insofar as it was the first time I had tried it for myself. And it was a singular one—insofar as it shall probably remain the last time I ever will.

The chief engagement of the current project is to attempt to present the reader with precisely what it was that made my travelling unique, and wholly unlike any other that has come before. This project will take us to the details.

The first thing that needs to be said with regard to the details is that I was not alone in my traveling. And I do not mean this as some Romantics and Transcendentalists have meant it—who have taken for their companions the objects surrounding them or the otherwise airier, more conceptualized notions of Nature and Human Solitude within it—nor do I mean it in the sense with which the religiously-inclined are apt to intend their unaloneness as being complicit with a vague and highly personalized idea of the Holy Spirit—a guiding, watching, probing, testing, protecting, nurturing, and ultimately sympathetic force of feeling through which one who is merely lonesome may be consoled of his or her position without needing even to verify it to anybody but himself. I am not one of those who counts himself to be anything but alone when he is, nor anything but not when he is not. And it is my opinion as a human being that the best kind of companionship available to us in this life is the human kind: a more fitful animal for a companion in all the earthly kingdom, there is none. It was my good fortune to have for my companionship three comerados of the finest order, who (though I would not speak for those who are capable of speaking for themselves) would probably agree with me on this point. There was a bond not unlike love between us, both before and after, that remains extant even now.

The other thing that needs to be said is that our trip was unsuccessful, in more ways than one; that we did not make it to Ocracoke Island, nor even so far as Tennessee; that on May 16th 2011, just after one o'clock in the afternoon, as the four of us rode in a line towards the town of Searcy, Arkansas along the shoulder of Rt. 16, Bill Cranshaw was struck by an automobile and killed instantly. It has become my main reason for writing all of the following to preserve the memory of him to the best of my ability and to present the story of these forty-five days, which came to be his last, which Paul Cavanagh, Hannah Liddy and myself were fortunate enough to have spent in his company, as my best effort to share with the reader the memory of who he was— or, rather, who he was *to me*—in the hopes that those of you who knew and loved him may come, perhaps, to know and love him more and better, and so that those of you who did not know him may not remain long unacquainted. I cannot tell the story of this trip from any perspective but my own. To assist me in the project, I have relied heavily upon my journal, which I maintained daily in the course of our journey, without which I do not believe I could have withstood to struggle to remember each day individually, without which much of my experiences should have been put at a further remove than I should have remained hopeful of regaining them.

I cannot tell now the extent to which I have written the following pages for myself, and to what extent I have tried to keep (you) the reader in mind. It is ever the test of a good story that where the distinction between the author's and the reader's experience ceases to matter is where one finds the question of whether or not it is any good belaboring. Suffice it to say: I have written the following out of the belief that we ought to be turned toward the same thing, you and I, with equal interest, and equal portion of ourselves. It is for this reason that I will apologize for nothing, and thank you, whoever you are, for your attention.

I shall conclude this introduction with a recommendation for how to proceed through the following narrative. Such navigation is best accomplished, perhaps, by simply opening it to any page and reading a little of what is there awhile. When your attention begins to flag, simply repeat this process. This will give you the best idea of what it was like to have been there, to have all of these pages as your memories. The greatest disservice to the reality of events as I remember them is done in the linear structure which my journal has allowed me to keep. It is almost impossible to communicate to the reader how jumbled everything becomes in one's memory when one is out upon the road with nothing to think about and nothing to do but ride on for the most part, to experience constantly the sights and scenes and sounds and smells and temperatures and events which are the components of a constantly unfolding story birthing a brand new world; and then to cease to move, quite abruptly, for reasons that can barely bear relating, because of events which are unimaginable to others and may become so, even to those who must keep them portion to their past; to try to come home again, knowing it is impossible, having lost the ingredient of your home in the attempted journey there. The event of Bill's death irrevocably changed the character of this trip in my heart and mind; in a manner of speaking, it changed everything, and continues to do so. And I have no doubt about the fact that had I not kept such a meticulous journal of the events which preceded his death, in complete ignorance of it, I do not know that I should have deemed the account of these forty-five days worth the trouble of reconstructing for the reader. The reason I have decided to try to tell about the bicycle trip in all its detail is not because I wish to explain the death of my friend to anyone. I shall posit here and maintain that the event of his death was arbitrary and meaningless; that all Death ought to be considered arbitrary and meaningless; that we ought never to be eased with the fact that a human being has died; that we ought never to die feeling that we have made our peace with the world; that nothing will justify death and nothing excuse it; that nothing will bring him back to the world as he was; that nothing may change the fact that he died. I should not have struggled so in telling about any of this for the pain of my labor to conclude with the conviction that the best thing should have been if we had never left home in the first place. The reason I have sought in this document to tell you about our bicycle trip is because it was nothing short of remarkable; because if Bill were here, now, I do not doubt that he would have enthusiastically said the same; because it was the only thing he ever did say about it. My hope is that these pages may only tell some of the story that four of us were there to experience; that they may preserve Bill a little in their telling and remind us a little of him as he was; that they may affirm each extraordinary day as having taken place; and may perhaps also convey something about the project of this life here upon this globe that we have not quite learned the full of yet. The universe remains as powerless to deprive the hearts of those who knew and loved Bill

Cranshaw of his residency there, as those hearts may be to bring him back. In the utterness of our powerlessness, we also have recourse to an immortal strength.

Nothing actually links the chronology of these pages in the order that I have arranged them except the efforts I made originally, upon the road, to remember things linearly. To convey to you at all the experience I have had revisiting this manuscript, and how constantly surprised I was to be reminded that certain events took place only after certain others, that certain places were not seen until others had been left behind—I should have to take these pages to the chopping block. The point of my saying all of this is: do not be deceived by the illusion of time's progression. Half the time you think it's moving backwards when it's really moving on.

What is more, I must repeat to you again that it should not be thought that I had articulated for myself all of this that you have just read before I had gone out and had my adventure. It feels somewhat anachronistic, maybe even dishonest, that this little article upon my own reasons for going should precede all of what follows from it. But perhaps there is some mystery behind one's reasons for writing that is just as mysterious as that for living life itself: we may seek the reason for ourselves, and never find it; yet the benefit of such a project may be painfully obvious to someone else.

Even after all of this which I have just set down to give my reader the impression that if I did not have a single reason for going upon this trip, I rather had a thousand—I must confess here as a kind of post-script to this essay that none of these aforementioned reasons, taken either by themselves, or in combination, were enough to make me actually set myself to saving my money for the express purpose of a bicycle adventure, or to examining all kinds of maps in my solitary hours in consideration of the way, or to thinking of the thing as an inevitable reality. It is easy to find reasons to travel; to go and travel remains the challenge. Such dreams and reasons for going as these I have spoken of herein may be the philosophical motivations for ten million behaviors amongst a million common souls alike—yet when it comes to the experience of one's singular life, I'm afraid they will not explain a thing. That I had never seen the country will not tell you why I ultimately set my foot outside my door; that I had no career lined up for myself immediately following my graduation from college will not account for the bike trip I filled a month-and-a-half of my time with; that I count bicycling to be the best means of transportation available to humankind will not justify my mounting mine, to ride a half-a-block, much less half-a-nation. If the reader will know the truth, I will say it plain: the mainest reason that I sought to cross this country on my bike had much less to do with anything which afterwards I could invent to justify it to myself than with a simple question that was put to me by a close companion. I did not go for me: I left my dreaming station and went to see what I could see quite simply because Bill Cranshaw, in a sincere way (one January evening, as Bill and Paul and myself sat upon the frosted banks of the Hudson River, watching the sun slip down into the favored pocket of the Catskills) asked me to come with him. And what is it, reader, which we have ever found clinging to our greatest resolutions, locked within our inmost hearts as the strongest motivator of our surest wills, but the wily and steerless carriage known as love? I went because Bill asked me to. I think we all did. And I wonder if in my response to him there was not something also like a question to which he then or afterwards eventually responded, and whether we are not all of us who wander merely void of will to cease, if only for the knowledge that we carry other wills in proportion and in place of ours, having, from the very first, given ours away.

www.ingramcontent.com/pod-product-compliance
Lightning Source LLC
LaVergne TN
LVHW041224080426
835508LV00011B/1075